A wealth of recipes, simple and exotic, that make the most of the delicious flavor and aroma of this unique ingredient, in harmony with fresh and natural whole foods.

Dear Cayman:
    I'm passing these gourmet recipes on to you — hope you find some great tastes surprises within. you are becoming a very good cook. I'm so proud of you

All my love,
Grandma

april 8, 2001

By the same author:
FAST VEGETARIAN FEASTS
HERB AND HONEY COOKERY
THE VEGETARIAN FEAST

GARLIC COOKERY

by

MARTHA ROSE SHULMAN

Illustrated by Rita Greer

THORSONS PUBLISHERS INC.
New York

Thorsons Publishers Inc.
377 Park Avenue South
New York, New York 10016

First U.S. Edition 1984

LIBRARY OF CONGRESS CATALOGUING IN PUBLICATION DATA

Shulman, Martha Rose
  Garlic cookery.

  Bibliography: p.
  1. Cookery (Garlic) 2. Vegetarian cookery. I. Title.
TX819.G3S58   1984   641.6'526   84-2675
ISBN 0-7225-0922-7

Printed and bound in Great Britain

Thorsons Publishers Inc. are distributed to the trade by
Inner Traditions International Ltd., New York

CONTENTS

INTRODUCTION

And scorn not garlic like some that think
It only maketh men wink and drink and stink.

Sir John Harrington

I began cooking at the age of seventeen and developed a passion for it immediately. I was home for the summer and every night would ask my mother for a recipe for a favorite dish. She would direct me to the recipe, help me with any techniques I might be unfamiliar with, and from there I would be on my own.

My mother had great recipes for spaghetti sauce, lasagne, and ratatouille, the Provençal vegetable stew, and since all of these contained a fair amount of garlic, this ingredient became a familiar one very early for me. I still have my mother's unmatchable garlic press, which she had bought in Rome when she lived there in the fifties. The sturdy metal gadget has traveled the world with me, and by now it must have crushed literally thousands of cloves.

Perhaps because I have always been so accustomed to cooking with garlic it did not occur to me until relatively recently that many people are not. Only a few years ago an English friend, also a passionate cook, told me that her parents had politely asked her to leave out the garlic the next time she cooked for them. I now understand that not only are many cooks and eaters unfamiliar with this herb but that they hold it in contempt; it is not the *"lilie extraordinaire"* in their eyes (and noses), but the "stinking rose," a plant that should be kept out of the kitchen and confined to the medicine cabinet. Throughout its long history, in fact, man has had a love-hate relationship with garlic. He has worshipped it as a god and has had great respect for its medicinal virtues, but he has also scorned it as a devil. His reluctance to accept garlic in gastronomy is probably due to the odiferous nature of the herb, for it is strong, and I imagine before toothbrushes and toothpaste were around it did weigh heavily on the breath, especially since it was probably most often consumed in its raw state. Thus the Roman nobles, who administered it in vast amounts to their soldiers for strength on the battlefields and in games, might have been justified in forbidding anyone who had eaten the bulb to enter the temple of Cybele, mother of Jupiter.

Despite man's mixed feelings about garlic, it did work itself well into the regional cuisines of the warm countries of the world where it is cultivated. And during the last fifty years it has become quite popular in the United States, not just in the ethnic communities where it has always been enjoyed, but up and down the coasts, and even in the Midwest and South. In some places its popularity has reached fad proportions, as in Northern California, where it is now celebrated annually at a garlic festival in Gilroy, "The Garlic Capital of the World."

The British have been slower to accept garlic. They have certainly had little encouragement — at least from the likes of Shakespeare, who talked only about its foul-smelling properties, as when Hotspur says:

Oh, he is as tedious
As a tired horse, a railing wife,
Worse than a smoky house. I had rather live
With cheese and garlic in a windmill, far,
Than feed on cates and have him talk to me
In any summer house in Christendom.

Or when Bottom says to his actors in *A Midsummer Night's Dream,* "And, most dear actors, eat no onions nor garlic, for we are to utter sweet breath." Until recently garlic was not a food touched by people of standing. The poet Shelley once wrote from Italy to a friend, "What do you think? Young women of rank eat — you will never guess what — garlick!"

But this attitude is changing as more people become exposed to different cuisines. The collection of recipes that follows is designed to help this progress along, for I am one of the world's great "lovers of the stinking rose." I hope that they will inspire you to keep a braid of this miraculous food, or at least a few heads, in your kitchen at all times — and not just for the purpose of fending off vampires!

CHAPTER I

ABOUT GARLIC

History and Lore

Although this is a cookbook and not an herbal (I have no intention of giving medical advice or of urging my readers to eat a clove of garlic each morning to treat this or that), I do feel compelled to discuss garlic's medicinal virtues; for they are well documented and extend far beyond the well-known lore that vampires cannot escape from their graves if their mouths are stuffed with garlic and more cloves are scattered around their coffins. It is indeed a miraculous healer: it cleanses the intestinal flora of harmful organisms, it is a natural vermifuge and expectorant, and it contains antiseptic and antibiotic properties. During both World Wars it was used to control gangrene, infection, and dysentery. In 1941 it was proved to lower blood pressure, and further research has shown that it dilates the blood vessels and reduces fatty deposits. So it can be useful in the prevention and treatment of arteriosclerosis and heart disease. It has also been shown to increase the body's ability to absorb B vitamins and to be effective in controlling blood sugar and cholesterol levels. Finally, it is a natural pesticide. No wonder garlic has been referred to as "nature's miracle medicine chest," "the camphor of the poor," "the poor man's treacle" and "the nectar of the gods."

Man has been aware of garlic's virtues for thousands of years. The plant, *Allium sativum*, is a member of the lily family and is thought to be native to the Kirgiz desert region of Siberia. It was brought to Egypt via Asia Minor by nomadic tribes and to Eastern Asia from India, whence it found its way to Europe via the trade routes. There is one record of an order by a Babylonian king, 4,500 years ago, for 395,000 bushels of garlic to be delivered to the court. The Egyptians, whom the Romans referred to as "Garlic and Onions," could buy a healthy male slave for fifteen pounds of garlic — and these healthy male slaves, the Hebrews, who were fed the herb every day for strength while they built the pyramids, were called "the stinking ones" by the Romans.

The Greeks ate garlic as a vegetable in its own right, not just as a seasoning for other dishes. Their esteem for the plant is evident not only in medical manuals but also in their literature. In Aristophanes' *The Knights*, soldiers are ordered to "bolt down . . . cloves of garlic. Well primed with garlic you will have the greatest mettle for the fight." We think that Moly, the plant used by Ulysses to fight off Circe, might have been garlic. In his medical manuals Hippocrates prescribes it against infections and intestinal disorders, toothaches, leprosy, epilepsy, and chest pains. The Greek doctor Dioscorides, who travelled with the Roman armies in the first century A.D., included garlic in his cures for somnolency, bloodshot eyes, skin diseases, inflamed feet, cough, spitting blood, dropsy, worms, the ejection of placenta and menstrual blood, poisonous bites, and for relief in childbirth.

The Romans seem to have had a more schizophrenic attitude towards garlic, for although the people worshipped it and its healing properties were widely accepted, the nobility still rejected it as a foul-smelling little bulb. They also considered the herb an aphrodisiac and ate quantities of it during the Festival of Ceres to celebrate its seminal powers. It was always an ingredient in love potions, including one that Virgil writes about in his *Moretum*.

Sixty-one of the remedies in Pliny's *Natural History* contain garlic. He lists all of the conditions above, plus asthma, running ulcers of the head, jaundice, "the iliac passion," scrofulous swellings of the neck, madness, phrenitis, catarrhs, hoarseness, pains in the temples, convulsions, ruptures, tumors, extracting arrows from wounds, liver spots, and epilepsy.

Garlic seems to have lost favor in Europe during the Dark Ages, but it emerged again during the Crusades, probably through contact with the East, and it began to be cultivated by Christian monks and herbalists. The herbals written in the Middle Ages, such as Culpeper's, are full of remedies calling for garlic (it was then spelled "garlick"); all of the conditions listed in the Roman manual are there, plus others such as poisoning by wolfbane and hemlock, hemmorrhoids and "cold diseases."

King Henry V of France was known as "*le Roi d'Ail*" (the King of Garlic) because he was anointed at birth with wine and garlic and popularized its use in his court, where garlic became known as a protection against the evil eye, as a stimulant, and as an antiseptic. It was normally rubbed on a newborn baby's lips.

Garlic became most popular as a folk remedy in France after the Marseilles Plague of 1721, when a band of thieves made a fortune by robbing the bodies of the dead victims, and it was rumored that they remained immune from the dread disease by taking a macerate of wine and garlic.

But garlic is not just an old world food. Indians in North and South America were familiar with the medical properties of the plant, which grew wild and saved many a settler from the effects of scurvy. The Indians, like the Greeks, ate it as a vegetable in its own right. Acosta, in Peru, noted that "the Indians esteem garlic above all the roots of Europe." Cortez ate it in

Mexico, and the Great Lakes Indians saved Marquette's exploration party from dying of starvation with it when they were making their way across that territory. The word Chicago derives from the name of the explorers' campsite, Cigaga-Wunj, which means "Place of the Wild Garlic."

The medicinal properties of garlic can be attributed to its extremely high sulphur content. It is broken down in digestion into diallyl disulphide, which is the odiferous agent, and allyl thiosulphinate, the medicinal essence. Heat destroys the enzyme that produces the odiferous agent, which is why cooked garlic tastes and smells less strong than raw garlic. Heat also reduces the medicinal efficacity. But food, after all, and not medicine, is our main concern here.

Buying Garlic
There are two varieties of common garlic, white-skinned and pink-skinned. The white-skinned bulbs seem to have the stronger flavor and are more widely available outside Mediterranean and Latin countries. The pink-skinned variety is slightly sweeter in flavor. I always look for bulbs with large cloves, no matter what their color, for the fewer and larger the cloves, the fewer one has to peel. There are usually about thirteen cloves of garlic on a head with large cloves, more if the cloves are small. Small cloves are also more difficult to peel. I have used large ones for these recipes, both the white-skinned and pink-skinned variety (they are interchangeable). *One large clove of garlic yields 1 to 1½ heaping teaspoons of chopped garlic.*

Before buying garlic, press the outer cloves to make sure that they are firm and solid. If they are not, the garlic is old and beginning to dry out and deteriorate. Only buy strands of garlic if you use a lot of it, as some of the heads will dry out before you get to them.

Giant Garlic. This is also referred to as "elephant garlic" and as the "sand leek." These large bulbs contain huge cloves, sometimes only a few per head. They are milder than the normal-sized varieties, with a sweet, nutty taste. There is something very luxurious about giant garlic.

New or Fresh Garlic. Freshly harvested garlic occurs in the spring in France, Italy, and Spain. Their stems are green, like those of onions, and their skins are soft. The cloves are not as easy to separate as those of older garlic, but once you get through the layers of thick, moist skin you will find sweet, juicy, tender cloves. They are especially good roasted whole and puréed (see pages 88 and 21) and are milder than the older variety. It is worth a trip to Italy, Provence, or Spain in early June just to experience this delicacy.

Powdered or Granulated Garlic. I only mention this to tell you not to bother. Better to use no garlic at all. This is processed garlic, and to obtain it the essential oils have been subjected to very high heat, thereby destroying the aromatic properties of the herb.

Working with Garlic

Separating the Cloves

Recipes normally call for a certain number of cloves of garlic, so the cook's first task is to separate the cloves. This, you will find, is no task at all, as you can easily get your thumb between the cloves and pry the outer ones loose. If you need several cloves you can smash the entire head with a rolling pin or the bottom of a jar. If a recipe calls for small cloves of garlic, use those at the center of the head.

Peeling

This was certainly the most unenjoyable aspect of working with garlic until I discovered the following techniques, which have eliminated the "garlic-in-fingernails" problem that always results from peeling by hand. The little cloves do still pose a problem because even with these techniques it seems I still have to peel the skins off with my fingernails.

Method 1. Place the garlic on a flat surface and crush with the flat side of a chef's knife. Do not mash the garlic, but lean into it evenly but not too heavily. The garlic will be slightly crushed, and the skin torn and loosened, so that you can easily remove it. If you mash the garlic it will yield a stronger flavor, as more juices will be released. This doesn't matter if you are planning to put it through a press, but for chopping, slicing, or simmering whole cloves you should crush them gingerly.

Method 2. Place the clove on a flat surface and hit with the flat bottom of a jar. The skin will pop right off. If you hit briskly and immediately lift the jar off without mashing, your clove will stay fairly well intact.

Method 3. If you need whole, uncrushed cloves you will have to peel with your thumbnail, beginning at the root end. Sometimes I squeeze the cloves a little between my thumb and the knuckle of my forefinger to loosen the skin.

Method 4. Blanch for a few seconds in boiling water, then refresh under cold water. Skin will loosen and will be easy to remove. This method is a good one for whole cloves.

Preparation

There are several ways to prepare garlic, and the way you choose depends on your taste and the recipe you are preparing it for. For years my mother's garlic press was the only utensil I considered using when working with garlic; I wouldn't think of chopping it. But then I began to learn more about this ingredient as I used it in different kinds of dishes. I began to understand that pressing garlic yields a stronger, more pungent flavor, and sometimes that is not what I want. Garlic's distinctive taste is derived from sulphur compounds that are released when the cell membranes are broken and which oxidize upon contact with air. The more violently the cell membranes are broken down, the stronger the smell and taste. So garlic put through a press or crushed and mashed in a mortar will be slightly stronger than garlic that is chopped or sliced and much stronger than whole garlic that is slowly simmered.

Using a Garlic Press. A garlic press yields the oils and "meat" while retaining the pulp. Since it is the pulp that is often responsible for indigestion, this might be the preferred method for those who are queasy about the herb. But as I mentioned above, pressed garlic is stronger because more essential juices and oils are released. It is preferable to chopped garlic when you wish to avoid biting into little bits, for example if you are preparing an uncooked recipe. And of course it involves less work than chopping. I still use it more than any other method.

Cleaning a garlic press is not fun. The only way to really do the job is to use your forefinger to scrape out the pulp. Also, scrubbing the outside with the rough side of a sponge loosens the pulp, which you will nonetheless have to lift out with your forefinger.

One way to facilitate cleaning is to leave the skin on the clove of garlic. The purée will be even finer, and the skin will prevent the lighter pulp from clogging the holes. All you need to do is pull the skin out and rinse with hot soapy water.

It is worth investing in a good garlic press, one with a hinged plunger that fits into the cylinder where you place the clove. Those presses with only two arms which press together — the shape of the pressing end is usually rectangular instead of round in these presses — do not do the trick. What you end up getting is a lot of crushed white pulp and hardly any "meat" or purée. Half the garlic will be wasted in these presses, which are normally sold in supermarkets and housewares stores. So go to a good housewares store and buy a garlic press made of sturdy metal. And by no means bother with the new plastic ones that have recently come on the market.

Mincing. The most important consideration when mincing garlic is to get it very fine. Peel the garlic and slice it lengthwise in very thin strips with a sharp knife. Turn it crosswise and slice again. Now, using a rocking motion, move the handle of your knife quickly up and down, holding the tip down with your other hand. Chop using quick little strokes until the garlic is fine. As you chop it will spread out; just keep pushing it back to the center.

Coarsely Chopping. When the pieces needn't be too small, use the rocking motion of the knife and omit the first step of slicing lengthwise and crosswise.

Chopping with a Food Processor. When a large amount of garlic is called for, a food processor fitted with the steel blade serves as a quick and efficient tool. Turn the machine on and drop in the peeled cloves. The blade will cut the cloves and push them out to the sides of the bowl. They are chopped as finely as the machine will chop them when all the garlic adheres to the sides of the bowl.

Slicing. This is a method I often use when simmering garlic for a long time in vegetable stews or when cooking with grains. Just peel and cut in thin or thick slices according to the instructions in your recipe.

Puréeing. This is a marvelous technique for obtaining a very smooth raw garlic purée. Pour about ¼ teaspoon of salt on your cutting board and place a peeled clove of garlic half over it. Take a fairly blunt knife (like a butter knife), scoop up a little salt and, holding the clove steady with your fingers, scrape the blade down the edge of the garlic at a slight angle. You will be scraping off garlic and breaking it down into a purée at the same time. The salt is instrumental in breaking it down. Continue to scrape until you reach the last little bit of the clove, which is hard to hold onto and purée at the same time. Either discard this or crush with the knife and mash to a purée.

Mashing in a Mortar and Pestle. A stronger, less refined purée can be obtained by mashing garlic in a mortar and pestle. Pound and mash the garlic, adding a little salt if you wish, until it reaches the desired consistency.

Cooking Techniques
Just as the flavor or intensity of garlic can vary according to how it is prepared, the way it is cooked will also determine its character.

Raw. Garlic is most pungent when left uncooked. I prefer it puréed or put through a press if it is going to be used in this state, or else puréed in a blender with soups or sauces, as I don't particularly like biting into little pieces.

Sautéed. I would say that I begin most of my garlic-containing dishes by sautéeing the minced or pressed cloves in a little oil. It is a sure way to make your kitchen smell good and to whet the appetites of those who might be around. It flavors the pan and the oil, so that whatever else you cook will be gently infused.

Sometimes garlic is added later in the cooking instead of at the beginning. This gives the dish a sharper flavor. In many longer-cooked dishes, like beans, soups, and tomato sauces I will begin by sautéeing half the garlic, then add the rest halfway through the cooking or even towards the end. This will give the dish a more pronounced flavor. When adding garlic at the end of the cooking you should use pressed or puréed garlic.

Slow simmering of cut cloves. For vegetable stews like ratatouille or vegetable braises, slow simmering of sliced or chopped garlic renders a mild, subtle flavor.

Baking. Sliced or chopped garlic can be added to vegetables, such as mushrooms, tomatoes, eggplant, and potatoes, for baking at fairly high heat. It will brown a little and impart a marvelous, distinct flavor. Garlic is also included in many vegetable dishes that are baked at moderate heat. It softens and perfumes the dish.

Whole heads of garlic can be drizzled with oil and herbs, wrapped in foil, and baked or roasted (see recipes, pages 21 and 88) until the cloves are completely soft. The pulp is then squeezed out and spread on toast or mashed to a delicious purée.

Simmering whole or slightly crushed cloves. Just peel the garlic and simmer in water. The length of time depends on the recipe. The garlic will develop a mild, sweet, nutty flavor and a soft, starchy consistency. This is a wonderful way to flavor a broth. I cook whole cloves of garlic with grains and it too makes a fine combination.

Flavoring oil for sautéeing. Heat cooking oil over medium-high or high heat. Add garlic, either whole, chopped, or put through a press, and cook until the garlic turns gold. Remove the garlic from the oil and proceed with the recipe. This gives the dish a milder garlic flavor than it would have if the garlic were left in.

Seasoning oils and vinegars. For seasoned oils or vinegars, macerate one or two cloves, cut in half, in bottles of vegetable or olive oil and vinegar. Salad dressings made with these will be mildly flavored. My mother keeps a cut clove, impaled on a toothpick, in her vinaigrette, and this gives the salad dressing, but not your breath, a subtle garlic taste.

Storing Garlic
Garlic will last a long time if kept in a dry place with plenty of circulation. Do not keep it in the refrigerator or wrapped in plastic. Hang strands of garlic on a wall, away from the stove and heater.

Garlic Breath
Just because you use garlic in your cooking does not mean that everyone is going to have garlic breath. I thoroughly disagree with a Parisian who told me that one should never use garlic *"en ville,"* that it is strictly a food for the country.

There are some people, however, who are more sensitive than others (that Frenchwoman was, needless to say, one of them). In any case, the best antidote to garlic breath is raw parsley. Chewing two or three sprigs will help considerably. Other high-chlorophyll greens also work, but parsley is the best. You can also brush your teeth with salt, a method one garlic-loving friend swears by. I have also found that sucking on a piece of lemon helps.

Indigestion
Some people do not digest garlic easily. A widely-used technique for facilitating digestion is to cut the cloves in half lengthwise and remove the green inner stem. This makes quite a difference and may allow many people who dared not partake of the delicious herb in the past to enjoy it with impunity. Also, as I have already mentioned, pressing garlic without removing the skin prevents much of the hard-to-assimilate pulp from getting into your dish.

How to Use the Recipe Codes
You will find in these pages recipes that contain garlic in small, moderate, and large amounts, and whose flavors range from subtle to strong. Choose them according to your own tastes, remembering that quantity does not always

correspond to intensity; for one raw clove of garlic pressed into a salad dressing or a mayonnaise will be much more pungent than several cloves simmered gently in a soup. To make it easier for those who have used this herb infrequently, the recipes will be coded ①, ② or ③; these numbers refer to the intensity of the garlic flavor, i.e., the pungency of the dish, ① being the weakest on the scale.

You will see by the way the recipes are coded that the number of the code does not necessarily correspond to the quantity of garlic. For example, most of the recipes that call for garlic that is not cooked will have at least a ②, even if they only call for one clove. The exceptions to this are recipes in which a small clove of garlic is specified, or recipes like Guacamole, where the raw flavor of the garlic, only one clove, will be absorbed by all the avocado.

Most of the recipes calling for more than one clove of garlic fall into the ② category. You will be surprised to find recipes with as little as 2 cloves in the same category with those calling for 2 *heads*; but if the heads of garlic have been simmered slowly, the dishes will not be nearly as pungent as those containing one or two raw cloves of garlic. Where there is variation, or where the size of the cloves of garlic can make a marked difference in the intensity of flavor, I have allowed the codes to range from one number to the next (i.e., ② - ③). The ③ category is for those very distinct dishes like Aïoli, or for dishes where the cooking time does not allow for too much mollification of a large quantity of garlic; or where, as in the case of Roasted Whole Heads of Garlic, though the flavor is in fact quite mild, garlic is the only ingredient.

Opposite: Herb and Garlic Bread (page 18), Cream Cheese Spread with Garlic and Herbs (page 32), and Spinach Pâté (page 26).

CHAPTER II

BREADS, HORS D'OEUVRES, SPREADS, AND LIGHT LUNCHES

The recipes that follow can be made ahead and kept on hand for delicious, healthy lunches, light suppers, or inviting hors d'oeuvres. I can't think of a lunch or light dinner finer than Hommos or Spinach Pâté (pages 26 and 28) spread on a slice of the Herb and Garlic bread (page 18), with a sliced ripe tomato on the side. I would be equally proud to serve many of these dishes as a first course or as part of a party buffet. Also, since most of them are cold, they make delightful picnic fare.

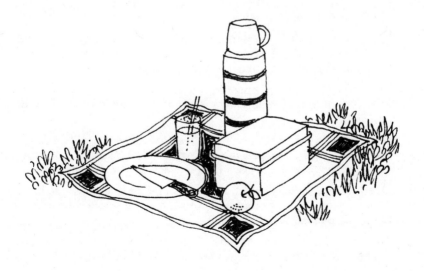

Herb and Garlic Bread

Makes 1 loaf

You can make any of your favorite breads into garlic bread by adding 1 to 2 cloves, sautéed in a little oil, to the recipe. Below is a mixed rye and whole wheat variety that I particularly like. This freezes well.

½ ounce active dry yeast
1 cup lukewarm water
1 tablespoon mild honey
½ medium onion, minced
2 cloves garlic, minced or put through a press
3 tablespoons safflower or vegetable oil
1-1½ teaspoons sea salt
½ cup plain yogurt
½ pound rye flour
1 tablespoon thyme
1 teaspoon sage
1 pound whole wheat flour

1. Dissolve yeast in water in a large bowl. Add honey and set aside 10 minutes. Meanwhile sauté onion and garlic in 1 tablespoon of the oil until onion is tender, and set aside.

2. When yeast is bubbly, stir in remaining safflower oil, salt, yogurt, and sautéed onion and garlic. Stir in rye flour, a cup at a time, and add thyme and sage. Fold in half of the whole wheat flour.

3. Place a cup of remaining flour on kneading surface and scrape out dough. Knead 10 minutes (it will be very sticky at first), adding more flour as necessary.

4. When dough is stiff and elastic, knead into a ball, oil bowl and place dough in it, turning once to coat with oil. Cover with plastic wrap or a damp towel and let rise in a warm place 1 to 1½ hours, or until doubled in bulk.

5. Punch down dough and turn out onto a floured surface. Oil a breadpan. Knead dough a minute or two and form into a loaf. Place in breadpan, seam side up first, then seam side down.

6. Cover and let rise in a warm place 45 minutes, or until dough reaches top edge of pan. Meanwhile preheat oven to 375°F.

7. Bake in preheated oven 45 to 50 minutes, or until brown and the loaf responds to tapping on the bottom with a hollow sound.

8. Remove from pan and cool on a rack.

Illustrated opposite page 16.

Tofu and Sprout Sandwich on Rye

——— *Makes 2 sandwiches* ——— ②

---

4 slices rye bread or other whole grain bread of your choice

3 ounces tofu

2 teaspoons sesame tahini

3 tablespoons tofu mayonnaise with garlic (page 170)

2 tablespoons mixed chopped herbs, such as basil, thyme, parsley, chives, tarragon, chervil

2-3 tablespoons minced pepper

½ teaspoon paprika

¼ cup alfalfa, mung bean, or lentil sprouts, or a mixture

Soy sauce, to taste

1 large ripe tomato, sliced

---

1. Mash together tofu, tahini, tofu mayonnaise with garlic, and herbs.

2. Mix in pepper, paprika, and sprouts (or you can reserve sprouts and top mixture with them).

3. Add soy sauce to taste and spread on bread. Top with sprouts if they are not already in the mixture. Serve open-faced or closed with tomatoes.

Pan Bagnat
————————————— *Serves 6* ————————————— ③

Pan Bagnats are as ubiquitous in Provence as pizza. They are, quite simply, a Nicoise salad on a bun. They are as delicious an everyday food as you'll find anywhere. My version, of course, omits the tuna fish and anchovies that are normally included in this dish.

---

1 cup Garlic Vinaigrette (page 172)

½ pound carrots, grated

¾ pound new potatoes, steamed until tender and sliced

6 hard-boiled eggs, peeled and sliced

20 imported black olives, pitted and cut in half

4 ounces chickpeas, cooked

1 pound ripe tomatoes, sliced

**6 large, hard whole wheat rolls, cut in half,
or 2 long whole wheat French baguettes, cut in half lengthwise,
then cut into 3 pieces**

1 cut clove garlic

1 head Bibb lettuce, leaves separated and washed

---

1. First make the dressing. Set aside 3 tablespoons.

2. Toss together carrots, potatoes, eggs, olives, chickpeas, and tomatoes with all but the 3 tablespoons of the dressing you set aside.

3. Rub cut sides of bread with a cut clove of garlic and dribble on the 3 tablespoons dressing. Place lettuce leaves on half the slices of bread and heap with tossed salad.

4. Dribble what dressing remains in the bottom of salad bowl over cut side of the remaining pieces of bread, add what lettuce remains, and close the sandwiches.

5. Press together well and wrap tightly in plastic wrap for a while before eating. They should be slightly soggy. Great picnic food.

Baked Garlic Purée

Serves 6 — ③

Friends were somewhat hesitant the first time I served this dish, but they followed my example, squeezed their garlic onto croûtons, and were pleasantly surprised by how mild and delightful it had become. Just as in garlic soup, the garlic is mollified by the cooking. It becomes an unctious, satisfying spread and a healthy substitute for butter.

This can be made in two different ways. The heads can be left whole and baked in the foil, or the cloves can be separated. It depends on how much you want to serve and in what fashion. I like the drama of the entire heads, but it's also nice to serve individual cloves.

3 heads fresh garlic

3 tablespoons olive oil or butter

3 sprigs thyme, or ¼ teaspoon dried thyme

Sea salt and freshly ground black pepper

1. Preheat oven to 325°F. Either separate cloves of garlic or leave heads whole, according to your taste.

2. Cut three squares of aluminum foil, double thickness if thin, large enough to thoroughly enclose one head of garlic. Place a head on each square and drizzle on oil or rub with butter. Add a little salt and pepper and thyme.

3. Seal garlic in foil. The edges should be tightly sealed, but there should be some space around the garlic so that it can expand a bit and simmer in its own juices.

4. Bake in preheated oven 1 hour. Remove from foil packages. I usually place the heads on a platter with croûtons and other crudités, and let my guests separate the cloves and squeeze the garlic out onto their bread or crudités.

Herb Butter

Serves 6 ──────────────②

¼ pound lightly salted butter

1 very small clove garlic, minced or puréed

1 teaspoon chopped fresh chives

1 tablespoon minced fresh parsley

1-2 teaspoons minced fresh basil or tarragon

---

1. Let butter soften and mix thoroughly with remaining ingredients. Place in a butter dish or mold, cover well, and chill until serving time.

Soy Pâté
Serves 6 ———————————————— ②

6 ounces raw soybeans, cooked until tender

2 eggs

½ cup milk

2 tablespoons brandy

2 heaping teaspoons Vegex*

2 teaspoons soy sauce

2 cloves garlic

½ teaspoon dried thyme

Pinch of allspice

Pinch of ginger

Freshly ground black pepper, to taste

½ onion, sautéed in butter or oil until tender

1. Cook soybeans until tender; drain.
2. Preheat oven to 350°F. Butter a pâté terrine, small casserole, or breadpan.
3. Purée all the ingredients except onion in a blender or food processor until you have a very smooth mixture. It's important not to have little chunks of soybeans. Stir in onion.
4. Transfer to prepared baking dish, cover with foil or a lid, and bake 45 minutes.
5. Remove from oven, allow to cool, and chill overnight. This can be frozen.

Vegex is a concentrated yeast extract. *Marmite* can be substituted.

Curried Lentil Pâté
Serves 6 ───────────── ①

2 tablespoons safflower or peanut oil

1 medium onion, chopped

2 cloves garlic, minced or put through a press

2 teaspoons curry powder

¼ teaspoon turmeric

¼ teaspoon chili powder

½ teaspoon cumin seeds

6 ounces dried lentils, washed and picked over

2-2½ cups water

1 teaspoon sea salt

2 eggs

¼ cup milk

¼ teaspoon ground ginger or ½ teaspoon grated fresh ginger

Freshly ground black pepper, to taste

1. Heat vegetable or peanut oil in a heavy-bottomed saucepan or soup pot and add onion, garlic, and spices and sauté gently until onion is tender, adding more oil if necessary.

2. Add lentils and water, bring to a boil, add salt, cover, reduce heat, and simmer 1 hour or until tender. Add more liquid if necessary. Remove from heat and drain.

3. Preheat oven to 400°F.

4. Purée lentils in a blender or food processor with remaining ingredients. Adjust seasonings and pour into a buttered pâté terrine or casserole. Cover and bake 50-60 minutes. Cool and refrigerate, or serve warm. This can be frozen.

White Bean & Basil Spread

Serves 6 ——③

---

1 cup fresh basil

2 large cloves garlic

6 ounces raw white beans, cooked

2-3 tablespoons tahini, to taste

Sea salt, to taste

Juice of 1 lemon (more or less, to taste)

Freshly ground black pepper

---

1. Combine basil and garlic in a blender or food processor or in a mortar and grind them together until you have a fairly smooth paste.

2. Add white beans and tahini and blend until smooth. Add salt and lemon juice to taste, and freshly ground black pepper. Chill.

3. Serve on croûtons or bread. This can be frozen but is better fresh.

Spinach Pâté
Serves 6 ———————————————(3)

3 pounds fresh spinach, washed and stems removed or 3 pounds frozen, thawed
1 tablespoon butter
½ onion, minced
2 cloves garlic, minced or put through a press
1 teaspoon thyme
1 teaspoon oregano
1 tablespoon wine or cider vinegar
3 eggs
½ cup skim milk
⅛ teaspoon freshly grated nutmeg
4 tablespoons chopped fresh parsley
2 ounces freshly grated Parmesan cheese
2 ounces freshly grated Gruyère cheese
¾ cup whole wheat bread crumbs
Sea salt, to taste
Freshly ground black pepper

1. Preheat oven to 350°F. Butter a loaf pan or pâté terrine and line with buttered waxed paper.

2. If using frozen spinach, thaw, squeeze out all the moisture and chop very fine, almost to a purée. If using fresh spinach, wash and stem, heat a large non-aluminum pan or wok, and add the still wet spinach in batches. Cook in its own liquid just until it wilts. Cool under cold water and squeeze out all the moisture. Chop fine, almost to a purée.

3. Heat butter in a heavy-bottomed pan and sauté minced onion until tender. Add garlic, spinach, thyme, oregano, and vinegar and cook, stirring, 3 to 5 minutes. Add more butter if necessary. Remove from heat.

4. Beat eggs together with milk and stir in spinach mixture along with remaining ingredients. Adjust seasonings and spoon into prepared baking pan. Smooth top and cover with a piece of buttered waxed paper. Cover with foil or a lid and bake for 45 minutes in a preheated oven, or until the top just begins to brown.

5. Remove from heat, cool, and unmold. Chill. This is good served with a Tomato Coulis (page 164). You can also garnish it with slices of hard-boiled egg. This freezes well.

Illustrated opposite page 16.

White Bean Purée with Fresh Mint

———— Serves 6 ————

1 tablespoon olive oil
2 cloves garlic, minced or put through a press
½ medium onion, chopped
½ pound white beans, soaked overnight in 3 times their volume water
4 cups water
Sea salt, to taste
Juice of ½ lemon (or more, to taste)
2 tablespoons plain low-fat yogurt or cooking liquid from beans
2 tablespoons chopped fresh mint
For serving: rounds of cucumber, crackers, bread

1. In a heavy-bottomed saucepan, heat olive oil and sauté garlic and onion until onion is tender. Drain beans, add them to pot, and add water.

2. Bring to a boil. Cook 1 to 2 hours, or until completely tender. Add salt to taste halfway through cooking.

3. Drain beans and retain some of broth. Purée through a food mill or in a food processor or blender, and stir in lemon juice, yogurt or broth, and half the mint. Add salt to taste if desired.

4. Place in a bowl and sprinkle on remaining mint. Serve on rounds of cucumber, or with crackers or bread.

Hommos (Middle Eastern Chickpea Purée)

Serves 6 to 8

1 cup chickpeas, washed, picked over, and soaked for several
hours or overnight in three times their volume water

Sea salt, to taste

¼ to ½ cup lemon juice, or to taste

2 large cloves garlic

¼ cup good olive oil

6-8 heaping tablespoons tahini

6-8 tablespoons plain low-fat yogurt

½ teaspoon ground cumin

Freshly chopped parsley for garnish

Halved black olives for garnish

1. Combine chickpeas with 5 cups water in a large pot, bring to a boil, reduce heat, and simmer 1 hour.

2. Add ½ to 1 teaspoon salt and continue to simmer another hour, until chickpeas are soft. Drain, retaining some of the liquid.

3. In a blender, food processor, or mortar and pestle grind together cooked chickpeas, lemon juice, garlic, olive oil, tahini, and yogurt until you have a smooth paste. Add more yogurt or some cooking liquid from beans if you want a smoother purée. Add salt to taste and ground cumin, and blend in.

4. Transfer to a bowl, sprinkle with parsley, and garnish with black olives. Serve with bread, crackers, or rounds of cucumber. This can be frozen.

Tapenade: Provençal Olive Paste

— *Serves 6* — ③

This makes a very special hors d'oeuvre spread thinly on croûtons. Serve it on a warm summer night with a glass of cool champagne or dry white or rosé wine, and let it transport you to the south of France. Traditionally tapenade is made with anchovies and tuna, but I think this is a robust and satisfying version. It is very salty and high in fat, so eat it sparingly. It is not an everyday food.

½ pound imported Provençal olives (Use Greek if these cannot be found.)

1-2 cloves garlic, to taste, puréed or put through a press

2 tablespoons capers

¼ teaspoon thyme (or more, to taste)

¼ teaspoon crushed rosemary (or more, to taste)

2 tablespoons olive oil

2 tablespoons lemon juice

1 teaspoon Dijon mustard

Lots of freshly ground black pepper

2 tablespoons cognac (optional)

---

1. Pit olives and mash to a purée with garlic and capers, using a mortar and pestle.

2. Blend in herbs, lemon juice, and olive oil and continue to mash until you have a smooth purée.

3. Blend in remaining ingredients and correct seasonings. Chill in a covered bowl until ready to serve.

Tapenade Barquettes
Serves 6 ③

---

1 recipe Tapenade (page 31)

6 eggs

3 medium-sized ripe tomatoes, cut in half

**2 medium zucchini, cut in half lengthwise
and then into 3-inch lengths**

Chopped fresh parsley for garnish

Radishes for garnish

---

1. Make Tapenade and hard boil eggs.

2. Peel eggs and cut in half crosswise. Carefully remove yolks and mash with Tapenade.

3. Turn tomatoes upside-down to drain 15 minutes. Blanch zucchini 3 minutes. Refresh under cold water and carefully scoop out seeds.

4. Fill eggs, tomatoes, and zucchini with Tapenade mixture. Arrange on a platter, garnish with parsley and radishes, and serve.

Caponata Provençal
Serves 6 to 8 ②

---

2 pounds eggplant

2 tablespoons olive oil

1 small white onion, sliced thin

2 large cloves garlic, minced or put through a press

1 red or green pepper, chopped

10 green olives, pits removed, cut in half

2 tablespoons capers, rinsed

4 tablespoons red wine vinegar (or more, to taste)

3 large ripe tomatoes, peeled and chopped

Sea salt and freshly ground black pepper, to taste

1 tablespoon chopped fresh basil

For garnish:

½ red pepper or 1 pimiento, cut in thin strips

Thin strips of lemon peel

Chopped fresh parsley

For serving:

Wide strips of green and red pepper

Small leaves of romaine lettuce

Whole wheat Croûtons (page 69) or crackers

1. Preheat oven to 450°F. Pierce eggplant several times with a sharp knife, brush with olive oil, and bake 20 minutes. Remove from oven, allow to cool; peel and chop.

2. Heat olive oil in a heavy-bottomed frying pan and sauté onion, garlic, and pepper over medium-low heat about 10 minutes.

3. Add eggplant and sauté another 10 minutes, stirring from time to time and adding oil if necessary.

4. Add olives, capers, vinegar, tomatoes, salt, and freshly ground pepper and continue to cook slowly, stirring occasionally, 20 minutes. Adjust seasonings and stir in basil.

5. Remove from heat and cool. Place in a serving dish, decorate with the strips of red pepper or pimiento and lemon peel. Sprinkle with fresh parsley and chill at least an hour.

6. To serve, surround with wedges of green and red pepper and small leaves of romaine lettuce for scooping, and have a basket of croûtons or crackers close by.

Cream Cheese Spread with Garlic and Herbs

Serves 6 ②-③

½ pound softened cream cheese
1-2 small cloves garlic, minced or put through a press
3 tablespoons chopped fresh parsley
3 tablespoons chopped fresh chives
½ teaspoon thyme
Lots of freshly ground black pepper, to taste
1 tablespoon lemon juice
Sea salt, to taste

1. Using a mixer, a bowl and wooden spoon, or a food processor fitted with the plastic blade, mix together all the ingredients until thoroughly combined. Adjust salt and pepper.

2. Refrigerate in a covered bowl until ready to serve. Serve on bread or crackers or with vegetables like carrots, celery, and cucumbers. Also makes a nice topping for small tomatoes.

Illustrated opposite page 16.

Opposite: Marinated Vegetables Vinaigrette (page 38).

Garlic Roquefort Dip or Spread
Serves 6 ————————————————— ②-③

½ **pound sharp Cheddar cheese, grated**

½ **pound Roquefort cheese**

½ **pound cottage cheese**
---
4 tablespoons dry white wine
---
1 tablespoon finely chopped scallion, shallot, or chives
---
1 clove garlic, minced or put through a press
---

1. Grate Cheddar into a mixing bowl and crumble in Roquefort. Add cottage cheese and blend thoroughly, using a wooden spoon, mixer, or food processor.

2. Add remaining ingredients and mix well. Place in a covered bowl and refrigerate until ready to use. Serve as a dip or spread.

Garlic Goat Cheese
Serves 6 ————————————————— ②-③

This earthy, herbed goat cheese can be further thinned out to be used as a sauce, as for Cauliflower with Goat Cheese, page 96.

½ **pound goat cheese**
---
1 clove garlic, minced or put through a press

½ **teaspoon thyme**

¼ **teaspoon crushed rosemary**
---
2 tablespoons plain low-fat yogurt (or more, to taste)

Freshly ground black pepper, to taste
---

1. Blend all ingredients together in a mixer, food processor, or mortar and pestle. Transfer to a bowl, cover, and refrigerate until ready to use. Makes a delicious spread as well as a topping or dip for vegetables like cucumbers, carrots, and celery.

Eggplant Purée I: Provençal

3 pounds eggplant, cut in half lengthwise and scored with a sharp knife

2 cloves garlic, puréed or put through a press

2 tablespoons olive oil

Juice of 1 large lemon

2 tablespoons plain low-fat yogurt (optional)

Sea salt and freshly ground black pepper, to taste

1 tablespoon chopped fresh parsley or basil

1. *For a roasted or broiled taste:* Heat broiler, turning it as low as possible. Brush eggplant with olive oil, place under broiler and cook 40 to 50 minutes, turning once, or until completely charred and soft.

2. *To bake:* Preheat oven to 450°F. Place eggplant cut side down on an oiled baking sheet and cook 30 minutes, or until completely soft and shrivelled.

3. Allow eggplant to cool and scoop out flesh. Discard skins and charred layer of cut surface.

4. Purée eggplant through a food mill, in a food processor, or in a mortar and pestle. Add remaining ingredients and mix well. Taste and adjust salt and pepper. You may even want to add more garlic!

Eggplant Purée II: With Yogurt and Mint

1. Use the ingredients in the Provençal Eggplant Purée above, but omit olive oil and increase yogurt by 1 to 2 tablespoons, to taste.

2. Omit parsley or basil and substitute 1 to 2 tablespoons chopped fresh mint, to taste.

Eggplant Purée III:
Baba Ganouch

Serves 4 to 6 ③

2 pounds eggplant
Juice of 1-2 lemons, to taste
1-2 cloves garlic, to taste
4 tablespoons plain low-fat yogurt
4 tablespoons tahini
Sea salt, to taste
Freshly chopped parsley for garnish
For serving:
Wide strips of red and/or green pepper
Cucumber sticks
Carrot and celery sticks
Crackers
Sliced whole wheat bread or Croûtons (page 69)

1. Grill or bake eggplant as in Eggplant Purée I (opposite).

2. Remove skins, discard seeds, and mash to a purée in a blender, food processor, or through a food mill.

3. Stir in lemon juice, garlic, yogurt, and tahini, and add salt to taste. Place in a bowl and garnish with chopped fresh parsley.

4. Surround bowl with red and green pepper strips, cucumber, carrot, and celery sticks, crackers, and bread. Use vegetables to dip or spread purée on bread or crackers.

Eggplant Purée IV:
Curried

Serves 4 to 6 ———————————————— ②

---

3 pounds eggplant

1 clove garlic, puréed or put through a press

3-4 tablespoons plain low-fat yogurt, to taste

Juice of 1 lemon

1 teaspoon ground cumin

2 teaspoons (or more, to taste) curry powder

Sea salt and freshly ground black pepper, to taste

Freshly chopped parsley or fresh coriander for garnish

---

1. Bake or broil eggplant according to directions on page 34.

2. Remove from heat, allow to cool, and scoop out flesh. Discard skins and charred part of cut sides.

3. Purée through a food mill or in a food processor or mortar and pestle. Stir in remaining ingredients and mix together thoroughly. Adjust salt and pepper.

4. Cover and refrigerate until ready to serve.

5. Serve garnished with fresh chopped parsley. Can be used as a dip for vegetables or as a spread on bread or crackers.

Cucumbers Filled with Herbed Cottage Cheese

Serves 6

---

2 large or 3 medium cucumbers

12 ounces low-fat cottage cheese

1 clove garlic, put through a press

1 teaspoon caraway seeds

1 teaspoon dill seeds

2 tablespoons chopped fresh herbs, such as basil, parsley, dill, fennel, marjoram, chives, thyme

2 tablespoons lemon juice

Freshly ground black pepper, to taste

---

1. Peel cucumbers if waxy and cut in half lengthwise. Scoop out seeds and cut in 3-inch-long pieces.

2. Mix together cottage cheese, garlic, herbs, lemon juice, and pepper. Fill cucumbers, mounding mixture high.

3. Serve as hors d'oeuvres, a salad, or a light luncheon dish.

Note: This mixture is also nice on wide strips of green or red pepper.

Marinated Vegetables Vinaigrette

Serves 8 to 10 ③

For the vinaigrette:

Juice of 1 large lemon

½ cup red wine vinegar

2 cloves garlic, mashed to a purée or put through a press

2 teaspoons Dijon mustard

2 sprigs thyme, minced

1 teaspoon minced fresh basil

1 teaspoon minced fresh parsley

½ teaspoon tarragon

Sea salt and freshly ground black pepper, to taste

¾ cup safflower or vegetable oil

¾ cup olive oil

1 small shallot, minced

For the vegetables:

1 green pepper, cut in rounds, seeds and membranes removed

1 red pepper, cut in rounds, seeds and membranes removed

1 small or ½ large cucumber, scored down the sides with a fork and sliced

½ pound mushrooms, cleaned and trimmed

½ pound new potatoes, steamed until crisp-tender and sliced

½ pound tiny ripe tomatoes, left whole or cut in half

Lettuce leaves for the platter or plates

Olives, radishes, and fresh chopped herbs for garnish

1. Mix together all the ingredients for the marinade except oils and shallot and blend well.

2. Blend in oils and stir in shallot. Toss with prepared vegetables and marinate in refrigerator at least 1 hour, tossing occasionally.

3. Line a platter or individual plates with lettuce leaves and top with vegetables. Garnish with olives, radishes, and chopped fresh herbs.

Illustrated opposite page 32.

Mushrooms Filled with Eggplant Purée
Serves 4 ────────── ②-③

1 tablespoon butter, safflower, or olive oil
1 clove garlic, minced or put through a press
12 to 16 large mushrooms, stems removed, wiped clean
¼ teaspoon thyme
Sea salt and freshly ground black pepper, to taste
1 recipe Eggplant Purée of your choice (pages 34-36)
Thin strips of lemon peel for garnish (optional)

1. Heat butter or oil in a large, heavy-bottomed frying pan and add garlic and mushrooms. Sauté about 3 minutes, add thyme, salt and pepper, sauté another 2 minutes, and remove from heat.

2. Fill with Eggplant Purée of your choice, stuffing cavities as full as you can and mounding purée above the surfaces of the mushroom caps.

3. Heat through in a warm oven or serve at room temperature. Garnish, if you wish, with thin strips of lemon peel.

Garlic Broccoli Stems

Serves 6

This is a much better idea than throwing away broccoli stems when your recipe only calls for the florets. It is one of my most popular hors d'oeuvres. People always want to know what they are. You can also add these to salads.

Stems from 1½ pound broccoli, peeled and sliced ¼-inch thick
½ teaspoon sea salt
1 tablespoon wine vinegar
1 clove garlic, minced or put through a press
2 tablespoons olive or safflower oil

1. Toss broccoli stems with salt in a jar and refrigerate several hours. Pour off whatever liquid accumulates and rinse.
2. Add vinegar, garlic, and oil and shake together well. Refrigerate for several hours. Place in a bowl and serve.

Artichokes à la Grecque

Serves 4 to 6

For the bouillon/marinade:
2 cups water
1 cup dry white wine
Juice of 2 large lemons
2 tablespoons vinegar
½ cup olive oil
2 cloves garlic
12 black peppercorns
1 tablespoon coriander seeds
1 bay leaf
4 sprigs parsley
½ teaspoon mustard seeds

1 teaspoon fennel seeds

1 branch fennel (optional)

½ teaspoon sea salt

1 large shallot, chopped

4 ounces raisins

For the artichokes:

4 to 6 large globe artichokes

1 cut lemon

10 to 12 sprigs chervil or 1 tablespoon chopped fresh parsley

1. Combine all ingredients for bouillon in a large flame-proof casserole or stock pot and bring to a simmer. Simmer, covered, while you prepare artichokes (10 to 15 minutes).

2. To trim artichoke bottoms, cut stems off and rub with lemon juice. Starting at base of artichoke, break off all the leaves by bending them backward.

3. Trim all the leaves around the bottom of artichoke like this until you reach the part where the artichoke begins to curve inward.

4. Cut off remaining leaves with a sharp knife. Rub continuously with lemon juice so that artichokes will not discolor.

5. Now trim the bottom of artichoke by rotating against the sharp blade of a knife so that all the tough green skin is cut away and the white fleshy part underneath the leaves is exposed. Rub cut surfaces with lemon juice and drop in a bowl of water acidulated with the juice of 1 lemon.

6. When all of the artichoke bottoms are prepared, drop into simmering bouillon. Simmer, covered, 30 to 40 minutes, or until tender. Remove from heat and allow to cool in marinade.

7. Remove chokes by carefully pulling apart at the center and scooping out with a spoon. Refrigerate artichoke bottoms in marinade for 2 hours, or overnight.

8. Drain off marinade, discard parsley and bay leaf, and place marinade in a saucepan. Reduce over high heat to ½ cup. Adjust seasonings.

9. Place artichoke bottoms on a platter or on individual plates and pour on reduced bouillon. Garnish with fresh chervil or parsley and serve.

Vegetables à la Grecque
Serves 6 ②

---

1 recipe Bouillon/Marinade (page 40)

12 small scallions, white part only

8 whole cloves garlic, peeled

2 medium-sized bulbs fennel, cut into eighths

6 medium or small carrots, cut in 3-inch sticks

½ pound mushrooms, cleaned and trimmed

1 pound zucchini, trimmed and cut in 3-inch sticks

3 tablespoons chopped fresh parsley

2 tablespoons fresh snipped chervil or tarragon

Radishes for garnish

---

1. Place ingredients for bouillon in a large soup pot and bring to a simmer. Simmer 10 to 15 minutes while you prepare vegetables.

2. Add onions, garlic, and fennel and continue to simmer. After 10 minutes add carrots. Simmer for 10 minutes and add mushrooms. Simmer 10 minutes and add zucchini. Continue to simmer another 15 minutes.

3. Remove from heat and cool in cooking liquid. Refrigerate several hours or overnight, or keep at room temperature.

4. Drain vegetables, place bouillon in a saucepan, and discard bay leaf and parsley sprigs. Reduce bouillon to ¾ cup over high heat.

5. Place vegetables on a serving platter or evenly distributed on plates, pour on marinade, and serve garnished with parsley, chervil, or tarragon and radishes.

CHAPTER III

GARLIC SOUPS

There are so many versions of garlic soup that they deserve to be set apart in their own chapter. Though the idea of garlic soup might strike you at first as unappealing, these broths are actually quite mild. Simmering garlic in water softens the flavor, and you will see that the resulting soups are subtle and very satisfying. They can be served quite simply or can be enriched with egg, cheese, or pasta. Most are served over croûtons.

When I was in Spain I found garlic soups on menus wherever I went. They were also easy to find in Mexico. In France garlic soup seems to be more a dish to be served in the home than in restaurants, for I have never seen it on a menu. Yet I have never opened a Provençal cookbook that didn't have a version.

One of the most inviting aspects of these recipes is their economy, ease, and simplicity. Some take no more than 15 minutes from start to finish, and the ingredients are rarely more complicated than garlic, water, herbs, salt, eggs, and bread. Cheese and pasta are optional.

There is no better nourishment for someone suffering from a cold, sore throat, or flu than garlic soup. Indeed, it is one of my biggest compensations when I'm ill. However, I enjoy it just as much when I'm feeling fine.

Aigo Bouilido I
(Provençal Garlic Broth)
Serves 4 ——————①

"Aigo Bouilido" means, simply, boiled water in the old Provençal language.
In Provence it is said that "Aigo Bouilido sauva la vido" — "Aigo Bouilido
will save your life." This light bouillon does seem to have restorative virtues.
It is especially good as a light meal. I have found several versions, each tasting
a little different. You will see that the basic broth can be further enriched with
eggs, croûtons, or vermicelli.

2 large cloves garlic, peeled and crushed with the flat side of a knife
2-3 cups water
1 tablespoon olive oil
1 teaspoon sea salt (more or less, to taste)
1 bay leaf and/or 3 leaves fresh sage
Freshly ground black pepper, to taste
2 egg yolks
4-6 croûtons
3 ounces grated Gruyère cheese (optional)

1. Place garlic, water, olive oil, salt, bay leaf, and sage (if using) in a soup
   pot, bring to a boil, reduce heat, and simmer 15 minutes.

2. Add freshly ground pepper to taste and adjust salt. Remove garlic and
   herbs.

3. Beat egg yolks in a bowl. Carefully strain in broth, beating vigorously.
   Serve at once, garnishing each bowl with a croûton and, if you wish, a
   little grated Gruyère.

Aigo Bouilido II
Serves 4 to 6 ②

---

6 large cloves garlic, peeled

4 cups water

2 x 2-inch pieces dried orange peel

2 bay leaves

5 leaves fresh sage or ½ teaspoon dried sage

2 sprigs fresh thyme or ½ teaspoon dried

Sea salt and freshly ground black pepper, to taste

4 ounces whole wheat vermicelli

1 tablespoon olive oil

4 egg yolks, beaten in a bowl (optional)

2 ounces grated Gruyère cheese (optional)

Method A:
1. Combine all ingredients except salt and pepper, vermicelli, olive oil, and optional egg yolks and cheese in a soup pot.

2. Bring to a boil, reduce heat, and simmer 20 minutes. Add salt and pepper to taste, strain, and return to soup pot.

3. Bring back to a simmer and add vermicelli and olive oil. Simmer 5 minutes, adjust seasonings, and serve.

4. If including egg yolks, beat them in a bowl and slowly whisk in hot soup. Return to soup pot for a minute, then serve, garnishing each bowl with grated Gruyère.

Method B:
1. Start by heating olive oil in soup pot. Sauté whole cloves of garlic about 5 minutes, or until golden.

2. Add water, orange peel, and herbs, and bring to a simmer. Simmer for 10 minutes, strain, and return to pot.

3. Season to taste with salt and pepper, add vermicelli, and proceed as above.

Aigo Bouilido III
Serves 6 to 8

---

6 large cloves garlic, skinned
6 cups water
2 leaves fresh sage
1 tablespoon olive oil
Sea salt and freshly ground black pepper, to taste
4 ounces whole wheat vermicelli
3 ounces freshly grated Parmesan cheese

---

1. Combine water and garlic in a soup pot and bring to a boil. Reduce heat and simmer 20 minutes.
2. Add sage, olive oil, salt and pepper to taste, and remove cloves of garlic. Place in a bowl and purée with a fork or a mortar.
3. Return to pot, along with vermicelli. Simmer another 5 minutes, or until vermicelli is cooked *al dente*.
4. Adjust seasonings and serve, garnishing each bowl with a little freshly grated Parmesan.

Aigo Bouilido IV
Serves 6 to 8

---

8 large cloves garlic, peeled
6 cups water
2 tablespoons olive oil
2 sprigs fresh thyme
1 large bay leaf
2 sprigs fresh sage
1 teaspoon chopped fresh parsley
Sea salt and freshly ground black pepper, to taste
6-8 croûtons
6-8 eggs

1. Combine all ingredients except croûtons and eggs in a soup pot and bring to a boil. Reduce heat and simmer 15 minutes.

2. Meanwhile poach eggs, and put each one on a croûton in a soup bowl.

3. Taste soup, adjust seasonings, and strain into soup bowls over poached eggs.

Aigo Bouilido V

Serves 6

---

2 tablespoons olive oil

6 large cloves garlic, peeled

5 cups water

1 small bay leaf

Sea salt and freshly ground black pepper, to taste

4 ounces thin whole wheat vermicelli

2 egg yolks

4 ounces grated Gruyère cheese

---

1. Heat olive oil in a heavy-bottomed soup pot and sauté garlic over medium heat until golden.

2. Add water and bay leaf and bring to a boil. Reduce heat and simmer 10 minutes. Add salt and pepper to taste.

3. Remove garlic cloves and mash to a paste. Stir back into soup along with vermicelli. Cook 5 minutes, or until *al dente*, and adjust seasoning.

4. Beat egg yolks in a tureen. Stir in hot soup, stirring until thickened, then stir in grated cheese and serve.

Aigo Bouilido VI

Serves 4 to 6 ———————————②

5 cups water
6 large cloves garlic, minced or put through a press
Sea salt, to taste (1-2 teaspoons)
½ teaspoon thyme
2 leaves fresh sage or ½ teaspoon dried
1 bay leaf
1 egg
4-6 croûtons

1. Bring water to a boil, and add garlic, salt, thyme, sage, and bay leaf. Reduce heat and simmer 10 minutes. Adjust seasonings. Strain.

2. Beat egg in a bowl, and then beat in the soup. Return to soup pot, heat through, and serve over croûtons.

Rich Garlic Soup with White Wine

Serves 6 ──────────────────── ②

---

2 heads garlic, cloves separated, skins left on

4 cups water or Vegetable Stock (page 60)

Sea salt, to taste

6 slices rye bread

3 egg yolks

½ cup dry white wine

Freshly ground black pepper

4 tablespoons chopped fresh parsley or basil

4 ounces grated Cantal or Cheddar cheese

---

1. Set aside one clove of garlic for later use. Crush remaining cloves with the flat side of a chef's knife.

2. Combine water or stock, garlic, and salt and bring to a boil. Reduce heat, cover, and simmer 1 hour. Meanwhile toast the rye bread, and beat egg yolks and wine together in a bowl.

3. Strain soup, and gradually stir half of it into wine-and-egg-yolk mixture. Pour this mixture back into soup pot, add freshly ground pepper, and adjust salt.

4. Mince clove of garlic set aside, or put through a press, and add to soup along with parsley or basil. Heat through gently.

5. Place a piece of toasted rye bread in each bowl and sprinkle on some cheese. Ladle in hot soup and serve.

Garlic Soup Madrileno
Serves 4 to 6 ②

The paprika gives a special touch to this soup.

1 tablespoon olive oil
1 tablespoon vegetable, sunflower seed, or safflower oil
6 large cloves garlic (or 8-10 smaller ones), peeled
¾ pound tomatoes, coarsely chopped
1 small bay leaf
½ teaspoon paprika
5 cups boiling water
4-6 slices bread
4-6 eggs
Sea salt and freshly ground black pepper, to taste

1. Heat oil in a soup pot and sauté garlic until it begins to brown — about 5 minutes. Add tomatoes, bay leaf, and paprika and continue to sauté 10 minutes over moderate heat, stirring occasionally.

2. Pour boiling water over garlic and tomato mixture, add salt to taste, and simmer, covered, 15 minutes.

3. Preheat oven to 400°F while soup is simmering. Place pieces of bread in a wide, oven-proof casserole and break an egg over each slice.

4. Adjust seasonings in soup, adding more salt if desired, and grind in some black pepper. Carefully strain into casserole, and discard garlic cloves, tomatoes, etc. (if you like you can press some of the contents through a strainer into the soup). Place in the oven and bake 5 to 7 minutes, or until eggs are set. Serve at once, with one egg per serving.

Garlic Soup with Poached Eggs, from Seville

Serves 6 to 8 ②

2 tablespoons olive oil (more if needed)
6-8 slices whole wheat bread
5 large cloves garlic, peeled but left whole
3 large cloves garlic, peeled and sliced
6 cups water or Vegetable Stock (page 60)
Sea salt and freshly ground black pepper, to taste
6-8 poached eggs
1 tablespoon chopped fresh parsley

1. Heat oil in a heavy-bottomed soup pot and add whole cloves of garlic. Sauté until brown, remove, and set aside.

2. Fry slices of bread on both sides in the same oil, until crisp, and set aside.

3. Add a little more oil if necessary and sliced garlic, and sauté about 2 minutes, then add water or stock and salt and freshly ground pepper to taste. Bring this to a boil.

4. Crush whole cloves of garlic already sautéed and set aside, and stir into water. Reduce heat and simmer 10 minutes.

5. Meanwhile poach eggs and place on croûtons in separate soup bowls.

6. Stir parsley into soup, adjust seasonings, and ladle into soup bowls. Serve.

Raw Garlic Soup with Grapes

Serves 4 ——————————————(3)

This recipe is only for the garlic fanatic. The garlic is uncooked, and the soup is a very powerful one — only to be eaten among friends, in my opinion. It is a creamy white soup with a strong garlic flavor, which the sweet green grapes mollify.

2 ounces almonds, blanched, skins removed
2 ounces fresh whole wheat bread crumbs
4-5 cloves garlic, peeled
2 tablespoons safflower or vegetable oil
1½ tablespoons vinegar (or more, to taste)
2 cups water
Sea salt, to taste
4 ice cubes
1 pound green grapes

1. Grind almonds and blend together with bread crumbs in a mixer or food processor.

2. Blend in garlic and grind together to a paste. Add oil and vinegar and mix together well.

3. Blend in water and add salt to taste. Add a bit more vinegar if you like. The soup should have a milky consistency.

4. Chill 1 hour and adjust seasonings. Serve over ice cubes, garnishing each bowl with a generous amount of grapes.

Rich Garlic Soup

Serves 4 to 6 ②

---

2 tablespoons olive oil

3 heads garlic, separated into cloves and peeled

5 cups water

1½-2 teaspoons sea salt, to taste

¼ teaspoon sage

¼ teaspoon thyme

1 small bay leaf

Freshly ground black pepper, to taste

2 egg yolks

Parsley and croûtons for garnish

1. Heat olive oil in a soup pot and sauté garlic about 3 minutes. Add water, salt, and herbs and bring to a boil. Reduce heat, cover, and simmer 1 hour. Remove from heat and strain.

2. Purée garlic cloves with some of the broth to moisten and return broth and puréed garlic to soup pot. Heat through again. Add pepper to taste.

3. Beat egg yolks in a bowl and pour in some of the soup. Mix well and pour back into soup pot. Heat through but do not boil, and serve at once, garnished with parsley and croûtons.

Sopa de Ajo Mexicano I

——————————————— Serves 6 ———————————————

---

3 large or 4 small *heads* red garlic, cloves separated and peeled

6 tablespoons safflower or vegetable oil

2 tablespoons olive oil

2 sprigs fresh thyme

1 bay leaf

5 cups Vegetable Stock (page 60) or water

Sea salt and freshly ground black pepper, to taste

Pinch of cayenne

6 slices whole wheat bread

2 ounces freshly grated Parmesan cheese

2 tablespoons chopped fresh basil

---

1. Set aside 2 cloves garlic.

2. Heat oils in a heavy-bottomed soup pot over low heat and add remaining cloves of garlic. Stew garlic in oil, along with thyme and bay leaf, 20 to 30 minutes over low heat. Garlic should be soft but not brown. Stir occasionally.

3. Pour off oil and reserve. To the pot add stock or water and salt and freshly ground pepper to taste. Bring to a boil, reduce heat, and simmer 20 minutes. Strain and return broth to pot. Add a pinch of cayenne and adjust seasonings.

4. Meanwhile brush bread slices with oil in which you sautéed garlic, and bake at 375°F until toasted. When you remove from the oven, rub with a cut clove of garlic.

5. Place a croûton in each soup bowl and sprinkle on Parmesan. Stir basil into soup, and ladle into bowls. Serve at once.

Sopa de Ajo Mexicano II

Serves 6 to 8 ———————————— ②

---

2 heads garlic, separated into cloves and peeled

6 cups water or Vegetable Stock (page 60)

2 teaspoons sea salt, or to taste

½ teaspoon ground sage or 2 fresh sage leaves

2 sprigs fresh thyme or ½ teaspoon dried

4 sprigs fresh parsley

1 tablespoon olive oil

Freshly ground black pepper, to taste

4 ounces whole wheat macaroni shells

3 egg yolks

6-8 slices toasted whole wheat bread (optional)

3 ounces grated Gruyère cheese

---

1. Combine garlic, water or stock, salt, herbs, and olive oil and bring to a boil. Reduce heat, cover, and simmer 1 hour. Add freshly ground pepper to taste, adjust seasonings, and strain.

2. Return bouillon to soup pot and add macaroni shells. Simmer 10 to 15 minutes, or until *al dente*. Beat egg yolks and carefully stir into soup. Do not boil.

3. Place a slice of bread (optional) in each soup bowl, top with grated cheese, and ladle in soup, making sure that there are plenty of macaroni shells in each serving.

Garlic Soup with Cumin and Cheddar

Serves 4 ────────────────── ②

---

6 cloves garlic, peeled and crushed with the flat side of a knife

3 cups water

1 tablespoon olive oil

1 teaspoon salt (more or less, to taste)

1 bay leaf

2 teaspoons crushed cumin seeds

Freshly ground black pepper, to taste

4 slices rye or black bread

1 cut clove garlic

2 eggs

4 ounces medium-sharp Cheddar or Cantal cheese

1. Place garlic, water, olive oil, salt, bay leaf, and cumin seeds in a soup pot and bring to a boil. Reduce heat and simmer 15 minutes.

2. Remove garlic and bay leaf, add freshly ground pepper to taste, and adjust salt.

3. While soup is simmering, toast bread and immediately rub each slice with a cut clove of garlic.

4. Beat eggs in a bowl. Ladle in half the broth, stirring all the while, and return to soup pot. Heat through but do not boil.

5. Place a croûton in each soup bowl and top with grated Cheddar or Cantal. Ladle in soup and serve.

Garlic Soup with Potatoes and Cumin

Serves 4 ——————————————(2)

---

4 large cloves garlic, peeled and crushed with the flat side of a knife

---

3 cups water

---

1 tablespoon olive oil

---

1 teaspoon (more or less, to taste) sea salt

---

1 bay leaf

2-3 leaves fresh sage (optional)

Freshly ground black pepper, to taste

---

4 medium boiling potatoes (about 1 pound), scrubbed and sliced fairly thin

---

2 teaspoons cumin, crushed

---

2 eggs

---

3 ounces Gruyère cheese, grated

---

1. Place garlic, water, olive oil, salt, bay leaf, and sage in a soup pot, bring to a boil, reduce heat, and simmer 15 minutes. Add freshly ground pepper to taste and adjust salt. Remove garlic and herbs.

2. Add potatoes and cumin and simmer 10 minutes, or until potatoes are tender.

3. Beat egg yolks in a bowl. Carefully beat in about half the soup broth. Return to pot, heat through but do not boil, and serve, sprinkling each bowl with Gruyère.

Garlic Soup with Tofu and Noodles

Serves 4 to 6 ───────────────②

---

8 large cloves garlic, peeled and crushed with the flat side of a knife

5 cups water

1 tablespoon olive oil

1 teaspoon (more or less, to taste) sea salt

1 bay leaf

4-6 ounces whole wheat or buckwheat noodles

¾ pound tofu, cut in thin slivers

2 tablespoons chopped, fresh coriander

---

1. Combine garlic, water, olive oil, salt, and bay leaf in a soup pot and bring to a boil. Reduce heat and simmer 20 minutes. Remove garlic and bay leaf and adjust seasonings.

2. Add noodles and tofu and continue to simmer until noodles are cooked *al dente* — 5 to 10 minutes. Serve, garnishing each bowl with chopped, fresh coriander.

---------- CHAPTER IV ----------

SOUPS

I rarely make a soup without adding at least a little bit of garlic. Sometimes it is just one small clove, which will accent the flavors of the vegetables. In other soups, like Pistou on page 62, a hearty Provençal vegetable soup enriched with a basil pesto, or the Minestrone on page 76, garlic holds a more important position. Some soups, while they don't call for the addition of garlic, are best when made with a Garlic Broth (page 60). In fact, I find that this broth better than chicken stock, the traditional stock called for in some of these recipes (see Egg-Lemon Soup, page 61). As it does in the garlic soups in the last chapter, the garlic loses its sharpness as it cooks, and you will not find it overpowering.

Most of these soups, with a salad and some good bread, make a meal in themselves.

Vegetable Stock

Serves 6 ——————— ①

6 cups water
1 onion, cut in quarters
½ pound leeks, cleaned, trimmed, and cut in large chunks
1 pound potatoes, scrubbed and cut in quarters
2 carrots, scrubbed and cut in chunks
6 cloves garlic, peeled
1 bay leaf
2 sprigs thyme or ¼ teaspoon dried thyme
2 sprigs parsley
6 black peppercorns
1 teaspoon sea salt, or more to taste

1. Combine all the ingredients in a stock pot, bring to a simmer, and cook, uncovered, 45 minutes to 1 hour. Strain. Keep broth on hand in the refrigerator or freezer.

Garlic Broth

Serves 6 ——————— ③

This stock can be used interchangeably with Vegetable Stock (above). It will obviously give a stronger garlic flavour.

2 heads garlic, cloves separated and peeled
6 cups water
1 bay leaf
2 sprigs parsley
2 sprigs thyme or ¼ teaspoon dried thyme
1-2 teaspoons sea salt

1. Combine all ingredients in a stock pot, bring to a boil, reduce heat, cover, and simmer 1 hour. Strain. Keep on hand in the refrigerator or freezer.

Egg-Lemon Soup

Serves 4 to 6 ②

4 cups Garlic Broth (page 60) or any of the garlic soups on pages 43-58, without the egg or cheese
4 ounces raw brown rice, preferably long-grained
3 eggs
½ cup lemon juice
Sea salt and freshly ground black pepper, to taste
4 tablespoons chopped fresh parsley
Thin slices of lemon for garnish

1. Bring Garlic Broth to a boil, and add brown rice. Reduce heat, cover, and simmer 40 minutes, or until rice is cooked.

2. Beat eggs in a bowl and beat in lemon juice. Slowly stir in a ladleful of the soup, then transfer this mixture to the soup pot. Heat through but do not boil.

3. Adjust seasonings, adding salt and freshly ground pepper to taste. Serve, garnishing each bowl with a generous amount of chopped fresh parsley and a thin slice of lemon.

La Soupe au Pistou

Serves 8 to 10 ③

This hearty Provençal soup gets even better overnight. It is very thick, and you may want to thin it out on subsequent days with a little water.

1 pound dried white beans, or fresh ones if available
2 tablespoons olive oil
2 large onions, chopped
3-4 cloves garlic, minced
1 leek, white part only, cleaned and sliced
3 carrots, chopped
1 pound zucchini, half minced, half cut in larger dice
1 pound potatoes, scrubbed and diced
1½ pound tomatoes, peeled and quartered
7 cups water
1 bouquet garni made with 2 bay leaves, 2 sprigs thyme, 2 sprigs parsley, and 1 stalk fennel, tied together
½ pound green beans, trimmed, and cut in half if long
Sea salt and freshly ground black pepper, to taste
4 ounces whole wheat vermicelli or broken whole wheat spaghetti
Small pinch of cayenne
For the Pistou:
4-6 cloves garlic, to taste
Leaves from 2 generous bunches fresh basil
½ cup olive oil
6 ounces grated Gruyère or Parmesan cheese, or a mixture
Sea salt, to taste
3 tablespoons tomato paste (optional)

1. If using dried beans, soak overnight or for several hours in three times their volume of water. Drain.

2. Heat olive oil in a heavy-bottomed soup pot and sauté onion and garlic until onion is tender. Add leek, carrot, the half of the zucchini you minced, and continue to sauté, stirring, another 10 minutes.

3. Add potatoes, tomatoes, and beans, stir a few minutes more, and add water and bouquet garni.

4. Bring to a boil, reduce heat, cover, and simmer 1 hour, or until beans are tender. Add salt and freshly ground pepper to taste. Remove bouquet garni.

5. Add remaining zucchini and green beans and cook 10 minutes. Add vermicelli or spaghetti and cook 5 to 10 minutes, or until *al dente*. Add cayenne and adjust seasonings.

6. While soup is simmering, make Pistou. In a mortar, food processor, or blender, pound or blend together garlic and basil until you have a paste or a finely chopped mixture.

7. Slowly drizzle in olive oil and continue to blend until you have a paste. Add cheeses, optional tomato paste, and, if you wish, a little salt.

8. Just before you serve the soup stir in Pistou and mix thoroughly. Alternatively you can mix a spoonful of the Pistou into each serving. The soup freezes well. The Pistou will also freeze well if you omit the cheese and add it after thawing.

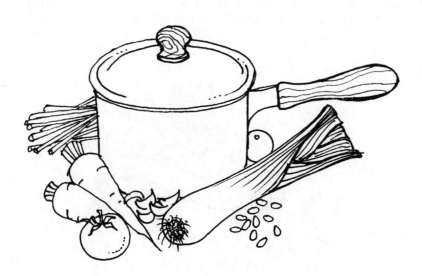

Creamy Leek Soup

Serves 4

1 tablespoon butter
4 large leeks, white part only, cleaned and sliced
2 cloves garlic, minced or put through a press
3 cups Vegetable Stock (page 60)
½ pound stale French whole wheat bread, crusts removed, and diced
Pinch of cayenne
Sea salt and freshly ground black pepper, to taste
½ cup plain yogurt or cream

1. Heat butter in a heavy-bottomed soup pot and sauté leeks and garlic over medium-low heat about 10 minutes, or until tender and aromatic.

2. Add Vegetable Stock and bread, bring to a simmer, cover, and cook 15 minutes.

3. Purée in a blender and return to pot. Season to taste with salt and pepper, and add a pinch of cayenne. Stir in yogurt or cream and serve.

Opposite: Aïoli Monstre (page 89).

Cream of Mushroom Soup

Serves 6 to 8 ①

---

2 pounds fresh mushrooms, cleaned and trimmed

3 cups water or Vegetable Stock (page 60)

3 tablespoons butter

2 cloves garlic, minced or put through a press

½ teaspoon dried thyme

½ small onion, finely minced or grated

3 tablespoons whole wheat flour

1¾ cups milk

2-3 tablespoons dry sherry, to taste

Sea salt and freshly ground black pepper, to taste

Chopped fresh parsley and sliced mushrooms for garnish

---

1. Set aside 6 attractive mushrooms to be used as garnish. Cut remaining mushrooms in half if they are large, leave whole if small, and combine with stock or water in a large saucepan.

2. Bring to a boil, reduce heat, and simmer gently, uncovered, about 45 minutes, or until mushrooms are tender and broth aromatic. Drain, retain broth, and reserve for later use.

3. Purée mushrooms in a blender, using broth to moisten.

4. Melt butter in a heavy-bottomed saucepan. When it begins to bubble, add garlic, thyme, and onion and cook a few minutes over low heat. Do not brown. Add flour and stir together with a wooden spoon to make a roux.

5. Cook this a few minutes, stirring, then slowly add 1¾ cups mushroom broth, stirring all the while with a wire whisk. Continue to stir until you have a smooth sauce. Pour back into soup pot, whisk in remaining broth, and simmer very gently 10 to 15 minutes.

6. Heat milk and stir in along with sherry. Season with salt, freshly ground pepper, and some of the parsley. Stir in puréed mushrooms, heat through but do not boil, and adjust seasonings.

7. Slice mushrooms, set aside and serve soup, garnishing with mushrooms and parsley. This can be frozen.

Purée of Vegetable Soup

Serves 8 ①

---

6 medium leeks, well washed and sliced up to the leafy part

1 tablespoon butter or safflower oil

2 large cloves garlic, minced or put through a press

2 medium carrots, diced

2 pounds boiling potatoes, scrubbed but not peeled

1 stick Swiss chard, washed and sliced

1 stick celery, washed and sliced

6 cups water or Vegetable Stock (page 60)

Sea salt and freshly ground black pepper, to taste (be generous with pepper)

¼ cup dry white wine

Handful of chopped parsley

6 tablespoons crème fraîche or yogurt

1. Heat butter or oil in a large, heavy-bottomed soup pot and sauté leeks and garlic very gently, covered, 5 to 10 minutes. Do not brown.

2. Add carrots, potatoes, chard, celery, water or stock, and salt and bring to a boil. Reduce heat and simmer 45 minutes to 1 hour.

3. Pass through the medium blade of a food mill. Do not use a blender or food processor, as you will not achieve the right texture.

4. Return to pot, season to taste with freshly ground pepper and additional salt to taste, and add wine and parsley.

5. Simmer gently another 10 minutes and correct seasonings. Just before serving, whisk in crème fraîche or yogurt.

Purée of Pumpkin Soup
Serves 4 ————————————————————①

1 small onion
1 medium clove garlic, minced or put through a press
1 tablespoon butter or safflower oil
2½ pounds pumpkin, peeled and diced
1 teaspoon paprika
4 cups water or Vegetable Stock (page 60)
1 medium potato, peeled and diced
Sea salt and freshly ground black pepper, to taste
1 teaspoon thyme
4 tablespoons crème fraîche, for garnish

1. Heat butter or oil in a large, heavy-bottomed soup pot and sauté onion and garlic until onion is almost tender.

2. Add pumpkin and paprika and sauté another 2 to 3 minutes.

3. Add water or stock, potato, and some salt and bring to a simmer. Cover and simmer 30 minutes.

4. Purée soup through a mouli food mill or in a blender. Return to pot and add thyme, pepper, and more salt to taste.

5. Heat through, adjust seasonings, and serve, garnishing each bowl with a spoonful of crème fraîche. This can be frozen.

Thick Purée of White Bean Soup

Serves 8 ②

---

2 pounds dried white beans, washed and picked over

1 tablespoon olive oil

2 onions, chopped

3 large cloves garlic, minced

7 cups water

1 bay leaf

2 sprigs parsley

1 whole leaf Swiss chard, sliced crosswise

Sea salt and freshly ground black pepper, to taste

Lemon juice, to taste

Croûtons (see opposite) for garnish

1. Soak beans overnight, or for several hours, in 3 times their volume of water. Drain.

2. Heat oil in a large, heavy-bottomed soup pot and sauté onions with 1 clove of the garlic until onions are tender.

3. Add beans, water, remaining garlic, bay leaf, parsley, and chard and bring to a boil.

4. Reduce heat, cover, and simmer 1 hour. Add salt and continue to simmer until beans are tender. Adjust seasonings, adding salt and garlic if you wish. Remove bay leaf and parsley.

5. Purée soup in a blender, in batches. Return to pot and season to taste. Heat through and add juice of ½ to 1 lemon, to taste. Serve with croûtons (see page 69). This can be frozen. Add lemon juice after thawing.

Garlic Croûton Slices
Serves 6

Several slices French or whole grain bread

Olive oil

1 large cut clove of garlic

---

1. If using thin baguette, simply cut into thin rounds. For larger loaves, cut thin slices into narrow strips.

2. Preheat oven to 350°F. Brush bread lightly with olive oil and toast until crisp in preheated oven. As soon as you remove bread from oven, rub each slice with cut clove of garlic on both sides.

Garlic Croûton Cubes
Serves 6

---

2 tablespoons olive oil

6 slices whole grain bread, cut into cubes

1 large clove garlic, minced or put through a press

---

1. Preheat oven to 350°F.

2. Heat oil in a frying pan and add bread and gàrlic. Sauté until cubes are coated with oil. Remove from pan and place on a baking sheet.

3. Bake in preheated oven until toasted.

Zucchini Soup with Dill

Serves 4 — ①

> **2 pounds zucchini, sliced ¼-inch thick**
>
> **1 small onion, chopped**
>
> **1 medium clove garlic, minced or put through a press**
>
> **1 tablespoon safflower or vegetable oil**
>
> **3 cups Vegetable Stock (page 60)**
>
> **3 tablespoons chopped fresh dill**
>
> **Sea salt and freshly ground black pepper, to taste**
>
> **Lemon juice, to taste**
>
> **½ cup plain yogurt or crème fraîche, for garnish**

1. Steam zucchini 10 minutes. Meanwhile sauté onion and garlic in oil until onion is tender.

2. Remove zucchini from heat and refresh under cold water. Set aside 12 rounds of zucchini and purée the rest, along with onion and garlic, in a food processor, through a food mill, or in a blender, using some of the vegetable stock to moisten.

3. Pour into a soup pot along with stock and stir together well. Reheat over medium heat and stir in dill and lemon juice. Season to taste with salt and freshly ground pepper.

4. Serve, garnishing each bowl with a dollop of yogurt or crème fraîche and three rounds of zucchini.

Thick Eggplant Soup

Serves 6 — ②

2½ pounds eggplant
Olive oil for baking sheets
2 tablespoons olive oil
1 medium onion, chopped
3 cloves garlic, minced or put through a press
5 cups Vegetable Stock (page 60) or Garlic Broth (page 60)
½ teaspoon ground cumin
2 potatoes, peeled and diced, or use potatoes from vegetable stock
Freshly ground black pepper
Juice of 2 lemons, or more, to taste
Sea salt, to taste
For garnish:
1 red pepper, chopped
2 tablespoons chopped fresh parsley

1. Preheat oven to 475°F. Cut eggplants in half lengthwise and score each cut side. Place cut side down on baking sheets that have been generously oiled with olive oil.

2. Bake 20 minutes or until shrivelled on the outside and cooked through. Allow to cool; peel and dice.

3. Heat oil in a heavy-bottomed soup pot and add onion and two cloves of garlic. Sauté until onion is golden and translucent, and add eggplant and remaining garlic.

4. Add a little more oil if necessary and cook over low heat, stirring from time to time, 15 minutes.

5. Add stock, cumin, and potatoes, bring to a simmer, cover, and simmer 20 to 30 minutes. Remove from heat and purée in a blender. Add freshly ground pepper to taste, the juice of 1 to 2 lemons, and adjust salt.

6. Heat soup through and serve, topping each bowl with chopped red pepper and a sprinkling of parsley.

Cream of Chickpea Soup with Coriander

Serves 4 to 6

½ pound chickpeas, washed and picked over

3 cups water

½-1 teaspoon sea salt

1 tablespoon safflower or vegetable oil

1 small or medium onion, minced

2 large cloves garlic, minced or put through a press

1 cup milk

2 tablespoons chopped fresh coriander

1 teaspoon ground coriander

½ teaspoon turmeric

1-2 tablespoons lemon juice, to taste

Additional sea salt and freshly ground black pepper, to taste

1 tablespoon fresh chopped mint and/or coriander for garnish

1. Soak chickpeas in water overnight or for several hours.

2. Bring to a boil in a large saucepan, reduce heat, and cook 2 hours, or until tender. Add salt. Drain and retain cooking liquid. Add enough water to measure out 3 cups.

3. Heat oil in a heavy-bottomed soup pot and sauté onion and garlic until onion is tender. Add beans, 2½ cups of stock, milk, fresh and ground coriander, and turmeric and bring to a simmer.

4. Cover and simmer 20 to 30 minutes over low heat. Remove from heat and blend until smooth in a blender. Clean the blades of the blender with the additional stock, and pour this back into soup.

5. Heat through and season to taste with lemon juice, salt, and freshly ground pepper. Thin out if you wish with more milk or water. Serve garnished with fresh chopped mint and coriander. This can be frozen.

Cream of Broccoli Soup

Serves 6 ②

---

1 tablespoon butter or safflower oil

1 small onion, chopped

2 cloves garlic, minced or put through a press

½ teaspoon paprika

2 pounds broccoli florets

1 medium potato, peeled and diced

3 cups water or Vegetable Stock (page 60)

Sea salt, to taste

Freshly ground black pepper, to taste

3 tablespoons chopped fresh parsley

1 cup milk (or more, to taste)

3 ounces freshly grated Parmesan cheese

1. Set aside 6 broccoli florets and steam just until bright green. Refresh under cold water and hold.

2. Heat butter or oil in a heavy-bottomed soup pot and sauté onion and garlic until onion is tender.

3. Add paprika, stir together, then add broccoli, potato, water, and salt to taste.

4. Bring to a boil, reduce heat, and simmer 20 minutes, uncovered. Purée through a food mill or in a blender and return to pot.

5. Stir in milk and parsley, add lots of freshly ground pepper, heat through, and adjust salt. Thin out, if you like, with more milk.

6. Serve, topping each bowl with freshly grated Parmesan and broccoli florets. This can be frozen.

Curried Zucchini Soup with Rice

Serves 6

1 tablespoon safflower oil

1 clove garlic, minced or put through a press

3 leeks, white part only, cleaned and sliced

2-3 teaspoons curry powder, to taste

2 pounds zucchini, chopped

4 cups water or Vegetable Stock (page 60)

Sea salt and freshly ground black pepper, to taste

6 ounces brown rice, cooked

½ cup plain low-fat yogurt

2 tablespoons fresh chopped parsley or chives, for garnish

1. Heat safflower oil in a heavy-bottomed soup pot and sauté garlic 1 minute over medium-low heat.

2. Add leeks, curry powder, zucchini, and a little more oil if necessary, and sauté 5 minutes.

3. Add water or stock and salt and freshly ground pepper to taste, bring to a boil, reduce heat, and simmer 15 minutes. Blend through a food mill or in a blender and return to pot. (If using a blender be careful not to overblend; you want to retain some texture.)

4. Adjust seasonings, heat through, and stir in rice. Serve, topping each bowl with a spoonful of yogurt and a sprinkling of fresh parsley or chives.

Rye Soup with Caraway
Serves 6 to 8

1 tablespoon safflower oil or butter
1 onion, chopped
2 cloves garlic, minced or put through a press
1 carrot, minced
1 stick celery, minced
6 ounces whole rye
½ cup beer
2 teaspoons caraway seeds
5 cups Vegetable Stock (page 60)
Sea salt and freshly ground black pepper, to taste
1¾ cups plain yogurt
2 tablespoons chopped fresh parsley or dill

1. Heat oil or butter in a heavy-bottomed soup pot and sauté onion, garlic, carrot, and celery until onion is translucent.

2. Add rye and 2 teaspoons of caraway seeds and sauté 2 minutes, stirring. Pour in beer and cook, stirring, until beer is absorbed.

3. Pour in stock, bring to a boil, cover, reduce heat, and simmer 1½ to 2 hours.

4. Purée half the soup in a blender until very smooth and whisk back into soup. Add salt and pepper to taste.

5. Stir in yogurt and serve, garnishing each bowl with a generous amount of parsley or dill. You need the bright green color of the herbs as a contrast to the dull brown of the grains.

Minestrone

Serves 6 to 8 ——————————— ③

This rich, luscious vegetable soup is even better served the day after it's made. The rind of Parmesan, which you can find at a cheese store (or cut it off the fresh Parmesan you have bought for the soup) is the trick for a deeply aromatic broth.

½ pound dried white beans, soaked overnight in 3 times their volume water

2 tablespoons olive oil

5 cloves garlic, minced or put through a press

1 large onion, minced

2 leeks, white part only, cleaned and sliced

2 carrots, sliced

½ small cabbage, shredded

2 potatoes, scrubbed and diced

1 pound tomatoes, sliced

4-6 ounces tomato paste

6 cups water, Vegetable Stock (page 60), or Garlic Broth (page 60)

¼ teaspoon celery seed

3-inch rind of Parmesan

1 bay leaf

1 teaspoon oregano

½ teaspoon thyme

Sea salt and freshly ground black pepper to taste

1 teaspoon dried basil or 1 tablespoon fresh

1-2 zucchini, sliced thin

4 ounces fresh green beans, trimmed and cut in half

4 ounces (unshelled weight) fresh or 2 ounces frozen peas

4 ounces broken whole wheat spaghetti

4 tablespoons chopped fresh parsley

4 ounces freshly grated Parmesan cheese

---

1.   Soak beans overnight or for several hours and drain.

2. Heat oil in a large, heavy-bottomed soup pot and add garlic, onion, leeks, carrots, and cabbage. Sauté, stirring over medium heat, about 10 minutes.

3. Add beans, potatoes, tomatoes, tomato paste, water or stock, celery seed, Parmesan rind, bay leaf, oregano, thyme, and *dried* basil (fresh basil should be added at the end of the cooking).

4. Bring to a boil, reduce heat, cover, and simmer 2 hours, or until beans are tender. Remove Parmesan rind and bay leaf.

5. Add salt and freshly ground pepper to taste, zucchini, green beans, peas, and spaghetti and cook another 15 minutes. Adjust seasonings.

6. Stir in parsley and fresh chopped basil and serve, topping each bowl with a generous amount of freshly grated Parmesan. This freezes well.

Winter Tomato Soup
with Vermicelli

Serves 4 ②

2 pounds canned tomatoes

3-4 cloves garlic, to taste

1 tablespoon safflower or olive oil

1 onion, chopped

1 tablespoon tomato paste

Sea salt and freshly ground black pepper, to taste

¼ teaspoon thyme

½ teaspoon marjoram

4 ounces whole wheat vermicelli

1. Drain tomatoes and retain liquid. Return liquid to can (or cans) and add enough water to fill. Put tomatoes through the medium disk of a food mill, or purée and put through a sieve.

2. Heat oil in a heavy-bottomed soup pot and sauté onion with 2 cloves of the garlic until onion is tender.

3. Add tomato purée and cook 10 minutes, stirring.

4. Add more garlic and the liquid from tomatoes. Add the tomato paste, salt and pepper to taste, and marjoram and thyme. Bring to a simmer and add vermicelli.

5. Cook until vermicelli is *al dente*. Taste again and add more garlic as desired. Serve.

Split Pea Soup
with Croûtons
Serves 6 ②

1-2 tablespoons safflower oil, as necessary
1 onion, chopped
2 cloves garlic, minced or put through a press
2 carrots, chopped
1 leek, white part only, cleaned and sliced
1 pound split peas, washed
6 cups water
1 bay leaf
Sea salt and freshly ground black pepper, to taste
2 tablespoons butter
6 slices whole wheat bread, cut in cubes
1 additional clove garlic, minced or put through a press

1. Heat safflower oil and sauté onion and garlic until onion is tender.
2. Add carrots and leeks, sauté a few more minutes, and add split peas, water, bay leaf, salt, and freshly ground pepper to taste.
3. Bring to a boil, reduce heat, cover, and simmer 1 hour, or until peas are tender. Remove bay leaf.
4. Purée half the soup in a blender or through a food mill and return to pot. Adjust seasonings.
5. Heat butter in a pan and add garlic and bread cubes. Sauté until cubes are golden (this can be done in advance). Remove from heat.
6. Heat soup through and serve, topping each bowl with a generous handful of croûtons. This freezes well.

Purée of Lentil Soup with Rice

Serves 6 — ②

1 tablespoon safflower or olive oil
1 onion, chopped
2 cloves garlic, minced or put through a press
1 pound lentils, washed
1 leek, white part only, washed and sliced
2 carrots, chopped
6 cups water
1 bay leaf
½ teaspoon thyme
Sea salt and freshly ground black pepper, to taste
6 ounces brown rice, cooked
3 tablespoons chopped fresh parsley

1. Heat oil in a heavy-bottomed soup pot and add onion and garlic.

2. Sauté until onion is tender, and add lentils, leek, carrots, water, bay leaf, and thyme.

3. Bring to a boil, reduce heat, cover, and simmer 1 hour, or until lentils are soft. Add salt and freshly ground pepper to taste.

4. Remove bay leaf and purée soup through a food mill or in a blender. Add a little more water if it seems too thick. Return to pot, heat through, and adjust seasonings. Stir in rice.

5. Serve, garnishing each bowl with fresh chopped parsley. This freezes well.

Opposite: Baked Whole Tomatoes à la Provençale (page 108).

Sopa de Cadiz – "Hot Gazpacho"

Serves 4 ③

2 cups water
1 pound tomatoes
2 tablespoons olive oil
5 cloves garlic, chopped
2 green peppers, chopped
1 teaspoon paprika
Sea salt, to taste
2 slices whole wheat bread, crusts removed
Freshly ground black pepper

1. Bring a pot of water to a boil and drop in tomatoes. Count slowly to 20, remove tomatoes, and run under cold water. Remove skins and seeds, and chop. Retain 2 cups of the water you boiled the tomatoes in and set aside.

2. Heat olive oil in a heavy-bottomed soup pot and sauté garlic until golden. Add tomatoes, green pepper, paprika, and salt and sauté 10 minutes, stirring occasionally, over medium heat.

3. Purée in a blender or food processor or pound together in a mortar. Add bread and continue to purée, add the 2 cups water, and blend until you have a smooth, thick purée.

4. Return to cooking pot, add freshly ground pepper, and heat through. Adjust seasonings and serve. This can be frozen.

Summer Tomato Soup
—————————— *Serves 6* —————————— ②

1 tablespoon olive oil
3 cloves garlic, minced or put through a press
1 tablespoon paprika
2 tablespoons dry white wine
3 pounds ripe tomatoes, chopped
2½ cups water, Vegetable Stock (page 60) or Garlic Broth (page 60)
2 tablespoons tomato paste
Sea salt, to taste
3 tablespoons fresh chopped herbs, such as basil, parsley, thyme, dill, marjoram, chives, chervil
Lemon juice and freshly ground pepper, to taste
½ cup plain yogurt, for garnish

Hot Version:
1. Heat oil in a heavy-bottomed soup pot and add garlic. Sauté about 2 minutes, then add paprika and white wine.

2. Sauté another minute and stir in tomatoes, water or stock, and tomato paste.

3. Bring to a simmer and simmer 15 minutes. Add salt to taste. Purée through a food mill.

4. Add lemon juice if desired, herbs, and freshly ground pepper to taste.

5. Serve garnished with a spoonful of yogurt and a sprinkling of fresh herbs.

Cold Version:
1. Proceed as above to the end of step 3.

2. Before you add herbs, lemon juice, and pepper, transfer to a bowl and chill 1 hour in the freezer or several hours in the refrigerator.

3. Then add herbs, lemon juice, pepper, and garnishes.

Beet Borscht

Serves 6 to 8

---

2 pounds raw beets, peeled and sliced

5 cups cold water

Juice of 3 large lemons

1 teaspoon sea salt, or to taste

1 tablespoon mild honey

3 cloves garlic, cut in half

½ cup plain yogurt or crème fraîche, for garnish

1 small cucumber, peeled and diced, for garnish

**Parsley, snipped chives or chopped fresh dill, for garnish
(optional)**

---

1. Combine beets and water and bring to a simmer. Cover and simmer 30 minutes.

2. Add lemon juice and continue to simmer, uncovered, 10 minutes.

3. Add salt and honey and simmer another 15 minutes. Remove from heat and chill.

4. About ½ hour before serving, add garlic.

5. Remove garlic halves before serving.

6. Serve topped with yogurt or crème fraîche, chopped cucumber, and herbs.

Gazpacho Andaluz

Serves 4

For the soup base:

1 pound ripe tomatoes, peeled

2-4 cloves garlic, depending on size and to taste, peeled

2 tablespoons olive oil

1-2 tablespoons wine vinegar, to taste

Sea salt, to taste

Freshly ground black pepper

1 cup ice-cold water

2 thick slices stale French whole wheat bread, crusts removed

1 small scallion, chopped, or 1-2 tablespoons chopped Spanish onion (optional)

½-1 teaspoon paprika (optional)

½ teaspoon crushed cumin seed (optional)

2 tablespoons fresh basil leaves (optional)

For the garnish:

1 small cucumber, peeled and finely diced

1 red or green pepper, seeds and membranes removed, finely diced

2 tomatoes, peeled and finely diced

4 tablespoons finely chopped onion

1 or 2 hard-boiled eggs, diced

2 ounces diced croûtons

1. Soak bread slices in water 5 to 10 minutes, or until soft. Squeeze out water.

2. Blend together all the ingredients for soup base until smooth.

3. Adjust seasonings. Chill several hours. The soup must be ice cold.

4. Serve soup and garnish each bowl with a heaped spoonful of the garnishes of your choice.

Blender Gazpacho

Serves 6 to 8 ②

Here everything is blended together into a thick, textured purée.

1½ pounds ripe tomatoes, peeled
2 large cloves garlic
½ onion, blanched 3 minutes in boiling water
1 carrot, cut in chunks
1 small cucumber, peeled and cut in chunks
1 green pepper, seeded and coarsely chopped
2 sprigs fresh parsley
3-4 tablespoons fresh basil
Juice of 1-2 large lemons, to taste
3 tablespoons olive oil
2 cups tomato or *V8* juice
Sea salt and freshly ground black pepper, to taste
½ teaspoon anise seeds
For garnish:
Choice or combination of:
4 ounces tofu, diced
1 ounces alfalfa sprouts *or* watercress
1 ounces sunflower seeds
½ cup plain low-fat yogurt

1. Blend together all the ingredients except garnishes, in batches, in a blender or food processor until smooth. Use tomato juice or *V8* juice to moisten. Chill several hours. Adjust seasonings.

2. Serve, garnishing each bowl with a choice or combination of diced tofu, alfalfa sprouts or watercress, sunflower seeds, and a spoonful of yogurt.

Chilled Tomato-Cucumber Soup

Serves 4 ——————————————(2)

---

1 long cucumber, peeled and chopped

3 cups plain low-fat yogurt

1 clove garlic, chopped

1 teaspoon paprika

3 tablespoons tomato paste (or more, to taste)

Pinch of cayenne

Sea salt, to taste

2 tablespoons fresh chervil leaves or dill, for garnish

---

1. Combine all the ingredients except garnish in a blender and blend until smooth. Chill at least 1 hour. Serve garnished with herbs.

---- CHAPTER V ----

VEGETABLE DISHES

Most of the recipes in this chapter are Provençal in spirit, for it was in Provence that I wrote them. How inspiring it was to have those strings of young, sweet garlic, "the truffle of Provence," hanging in my kitchen, to add to tomatoes, eggplant, artichokes, or whatever other delightful vegetables we carried home in baskets from neighboring markets. Occasionally I would make a curry, but more often the herbs that grew right outside my door would inspire the vegetable dishes we ate, sometimes as hors d'oeuvres, sometimes as side dishes, and often as the main attraction. You will see from what follows that tomatoes, mushrooms, eggplant, and artichokes seem to welcome garlic best of all, and that potatoes, peppers, and zucchini are a close second. But that does not exclude other vegetables; indeed, I hope this chapter inspires you to experiment. The recipes shouldn't dictate. If one vegetable is out of season and the recipe is tempting, try using another — broccoli instead of green beans, for instance, or chard instead of spinach. You might also wish to vary the quantities of garlic, and also the cooking times, as I might like my vegetables cooked more or less than you do.

Charcoal-Roasted Whole Garlic

Serves 4 ——————————— ③

This is especially nice if you happen to be grilling something else. All you do is throw the prepared garlic on the coals.

---

2 whole heads garlic (or more, to taste)
Olive oil

---

1. Brush heads of garlic with olive oil and place directly on hot coals of a fire that is no longer flaming. (You can baste the garlic a few times, but I find this unnecessary.)

2. When they are brown, or even charred, remove from fire and allow to cool. The skins will be hard and perhaps blackened, but inside the flesh will be tender.

3. Break off cloves and push out garlic. Serve on bread or just by itself as a side dish.

Aïoli Monstre
Serves a crowd

This is one of those festive Provencal dishes one sees at special occasions. During the grape harvest at Domaine Tempier, one of my favorite vineyards in the south of France, this is often served to celebrate the end of the harvest. Aïoli is sometimes called "Provençal butter."

---

1 recipe Aïoli (Garlic Mayonnaise — page 169)

2-4 artichokes, trimmed, steamed until tender, then cut in quarters and chokes removed

1 pound potatoes, steamed until tender and sliced

2 zucchini, cut into spears

1 small cauliflower, broken into florets and briefly steamed

1 small broccoli, broken into florets and briefly steamed

½ pound carrots, cut into spears

1 bunch radishes, trimmed

2 sweet potatoes, steamed until tender and sliced (optional)

Other vegetables in season, such as tomatoes, green beans, asparagus (Steam green vegetables until crisp-tender.)

---

1. Prepare Aïoli and refrigerate until ready to serve.

2. This can be served rustically, with vegetables in separate bowls and Aïoli in a large bowl. Pass Aïoli and let everyone take a portion, then pass the vegetables.

3. Or you can make a large, decorative platter and place the Aïoli in the middle or in mounds interspersed among the vegetables. Serve as an hors d'oeuvre or pass around as part of the meal.

Illustrated opposite page 64.

Ratatouille

Serves 6 ②

A collection of garlic recipes would not be complete without ratatouille, the slowly cooked vegetable stew from Provence. I have eaten the best ones in this region, and have concluded that in addition to the superb ingredients that grow in the area, the secret to these great ratatouilles is the earthenware pots in which they are cooked. These are easy enough to come by (they needn't be from Provence), and set over an asbestos pad they allow for the slow cooking that allows all of the heady aromas and flavors to develop to their utmost.

1 pound eggplant, diced

2 onions, sliced

4 cloves garlic, sliced or chopped

3-4 tablespoons olive oil

2 sweet green or red peppers, seeded and sliced

1 pound zucchini, sliced, or if very large, diced

1 pound tomatoes, peeled and sliced

1 teaspoon thyme

1 tablespoon chopped fresh basil or 1 teaspoon dried

Sea salt and freshly ground black pepper, to taste

1. Salt diced eggplant and let sit while you prepare the other vegetables.

2. Heat oil over medium-low heat in a heavy-bottomed, preferably earthenware, casserole and gently sauté onions and garlic until onion is tender. Add sweet peppers and sauté for a few minutes.

3. Rinse eggplant and pat dry with a towel. Add to pot along with zucchini, and stir to coat thoroughly with oil. Add a bit more oil if necessary. Add some salt, cover pot, and cook over a very low heat 45 minutes to 1 hour, stirring from time to time.

4. Add tomatoes and herbs, and continue to cook, uncovered, another 10 to 15 minutes, stirring occasionally. Add salt to taste and plenty of freshly ground pepper. You may also want to add more herbs or a bit of cayenne pepper. Serve hot or cold. It is even better the next day. This freezes well.

Artichokes Stewed with Tomatoes and Wine

Serves 4 to 6

4-6 artichokes

Juice of 1 lemon

1 tablespoon olive oil

1 small onion, minced

4 cloves garlic, minced

1 carrot, minced

1 stick celery, minced

1 pound tomatoes, chopped

1 cup dry white wine

1 bay leaf

2 sprigs parsley

Sea salt and freshly ground black pepper

1. Trim artichokes, cut into quarters, remove chokes, and drop into a bowl of acidulated water (use the lemon juice for this).

2. Heat oil in a large, heavy-bottomed, lidded casserole and sauté onion with garlic, carrot, and celery until onion becomes translucent.

3. Add tomatoes and bring to a simmer. Cook for 5 minutes and add wine, bay leaf, parsley, salt and pepper, and artichokes.

4. Bring back to a simmer, cover, reduce heat, and simmer 40 minutes, or until artichokes are tender. Adjust seasonings and serve with the liquid spooned over artichokes.

Whole Artichokes Braised in Wine

Serves 4 to 6 ——— ①

4-6 artichokes, trimmed
Juice of 1 lemon
1½ cups dry white wine
½ cup Vegetable Stock (page 60) or water
1 tablespoon olive oil
8 cloves garlic, cut in half
3 slices onion
1 carrot, sliced
1 bay leaf
Sea salt and freshly ground black pepper
½ lemon, sliced

1. Trim artichokes. Place in a bowl of water acidulated with lemon juice.
2. Combine remaining ingredients in a large, lidded casserole and bring to a simmer.
3. Place artichokes in the casserole upside down, cover, and simmer 45 minutes, or until tender. Serve hot or at room temperature.

Artichokes with Garlic and Parsley

Serves 4 ——— ②

8 very small purple artichokes or 4 larger artichokes
4 large cloves garlic, thinly sliced
1 cup minced fresh parsley
Sea salt and freshly ground black pepper

1½ cups dry white wine
3 additional cloves garlic, cut in half or thirds
½ small onion, sliced
1 bay leaf
1 teaspoon black peppercorns
Sea salt
1 tablespoon olive oil

1. Trim artichokes and scoop out chokes. Fill cavities with alternating layers of the thinly sliced garlic and the parsley, stuffing them as full as you can with parsley. Sprinkle with salt and pepper and place in a flameproof casserole.

2. Add wine and remaining ingredients to casserole and bring to a simmer. Cover and simmer 30 to 40 minutes, or until tender.

3. As you eat these artichokes, the flavor of the garlic intensifies the closer you get to the heart.

Baked Mushroom Caps

Serves 4

1 pound large mushrooms, cleaned, stems removed
3 large cloves garlic, chopped
4 tablespoons olive oil
½ teaspoon thyme
¼ teaspoon rosemary
Sea salt and freshly ground black pepper
Fresh chopped parsley

1. Preheat oven to 400°F. Place mushrooms in an oiled baking dish, top side down. Sprinkle with garlic and herbs, salt and freshly ground pepper, and olive oil.

2. Bake 20 minutes, or until tender, basting with juices in the pan every 5 minutes.

3. Serve garnished with parsley.

Sautéed Mushrooms
Serves 4 ——————————————②

This is marvelous with Polenta (page 123) or over any cooked grains.

1-1½ pounds mushrooms, cleaned, trimmed, and sliced
1 tablespoon butter
5 scallions, white part only, or 2 medium shallots, minced
2 large cloves garlic, minced or put through a press
4 tablespoons dry white wine
½ teaspoon thyme
¼ teaspoon crushed rosemary
Sea salt and freshly ground black pepper, to taste
Additional herbs, to taste

1. Heat butter in a large, heavy-bottomed frying pan and add onions or shallots. Sauté until they begin to soften, about 2 minutes, and add mushrooms and garlic.

2. Sauté over medium heat about 5 minutes and pour in wine.

3. Add herbs, turn up heat, and cook, stirring, until most of the wine has evaporated but you still have mushroom juices in the pan. Add salt and pepper to taste, remove from heat, and serve.

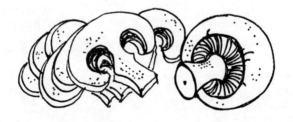

Toasts Champignons

Serves 4 ②

---

4 slices toasted whole wheat bread

Butter for the bread

1 tablespoon butter or olive oil for the mushrooms

1 teaspoon dried thyme or rosemary, or a combination

½ pound mushrooms, cleaned and thickly sliced

2 cloves garlic, minced or put through a press

4 tablespoons dry white wine

Sea salt and freshly ground black pepper, to taste

2 tablespoons scallion tops or chopped chives

1. Butter toast and keep warm.

2. Heat oil or butter in a heavy-bottomed frying pan or wok and add mushrooms and herbs.

3. Sauté 10 minutes over medium heat, stirring, and add garlic and white wine.

4. Cook, stirring, about 5 more minutes, turning heat high towards the end, until liquid evaporates.

5. Add salt and pepper to taste, and scallion tops or chives. Cook another minute.

6. Place toast on separate plates and pile mushrooms on top. Serve at once.

Cauliflower Gratin with Goat Cheese Sauce

Serves 6 ①

This dish can be assembled several hours in advance and popped into the oven 10 to 15 minutes before serving.

1 large cauliflower or two small ones, broken into florets
3 tablespoons olive oil or safflower oil
½ pound goat cheese, as soft and salt-free as you can find
½ cup low-fat milk or plain yogurt
1 clove garlic
¼ teaspoon thyme
Freshly ground black pepper, to taste

1. Preheat oven to 450°F.

2. Steam cauliflower for 10 minutes, drain, and toss with 2 tablespoons of the oil in an oiled gratin dish.

3. In a food processor fitted with the steel blade, or in a bowl using a wooden spoon, or in a mixer, mash goat cheese and mix with garlic, milk or yogurt, thyme, and freshly ground pepper. Spread over cauliflower. At this point the dish can be set aside.

4. Just before baking, drizzle with 1 tablespoon oil. Place in oven and bake for 10 to 15 minutes, or until dish is sizzling. Serve at once.

Hot Cauliflower Curry

Serves 4 to 6 ③

For the cauliflower and curry paste:
3-6 cloves garlic, to taste
1-inch piece of fresh ginger, peeled and minced or grated
½ teaspoon paprika
½ teaspoon cumin
½ teaspoon turmeric

¼-½ teaspoon salt

Juice of ½ lemon

1 cauliflower, broken into florets

For the sauce:

1 tablespoon butter or safflower or peanut oil

½ small onion, finely chopped

2 cloves garlic, minced

1-inch piece of fresh ginger, peeled and grated or finely minced

1 teaspoon cumin seeds

6 whole cloves

6 black peppercorns

1-inch cinnamon stick, crumbled

½ teaspoon cardamom seeds

10 almonds, blanched

2 tomatoes, chopped

1 cup plain low-fat yogurt

2-3 tablespoons chopped fresh coriander

1. Grind together all the ingredients for paste except cauliflower in a mortar and pestle, spice mill, or food processor. Moisten with lemon juice.

2. Dip florets of cauliflower into paste and place on a steamer above boiling water. Cover and steam 10 to 15 minutes.

3. Meanwhile make the sauce. Grind together ginger, spices, and almonds. Sauté onion and garlic in oil or butter until onion is tender.

4. Add spices, tomatoes, and a little salt. Cook a few minutes over medium heat, then turn heat down very low and slowly stir in yogurt.

5. Place cauliflower in a warm serving dish and pour on sauce. Garnish with fresh coriander and serve.

Italian Style Broccoli
Serves 4 to 6

1½-2 pounds broccoli, broken into florets
1 tablespoon olive oil
1 clove garlic, minced or put through a press
1 small dried hot red pepper, crumbled
2 tablespoons dry white wine

1. Steam broccoli 10 minutes, or until tender and still bright green. Refresh under cold water.

2. Heat olive oil over medium heat and sauté garlic and red pepper 2 minutes. Add broccoli and wine and sauté, stirring, another 3 to 5 minutes. Serve.

Roasted Eggplant with Garlic and Herbs

Serves 4 to 6

3 medium eggplants
3 cloves garlic, minced
½ cup chopped fresh parsley
1 teaspoon chopped fresh rosemary or ½ teaspoon crumbled dried rosemary
Sea salt and freshly ground black pepper, to taste
3 tablespoons olive oil
Lemon juice, to taste
Thin slices of lemon, for garnish

1. Cut the eggplant in half lengthwise, and make two lengthwise slits down the cut side of each half.

2. Mix together garlic, parsley, and rosemary, add freshly ground pepper, and fill slits with this mixture. Salt eggplant lightly and drizzle on some olive oil. Cover and chill 2 hours.

3. Make a wood or charcoal fire, or preheat oven to 350°F. When the fire dies down, grill eggplant, basting regularly with olive oil, until tender. Or place cut side down in an oiled baking dish and bake 1 hour, basting from time to time, in preheated oven. Turn eggplant cut side up for the last quarter hour and baste with juices in pan.

4. Sprinkle on some lemon juice, garnish with thin rounds of lemons, and serve.

Eggplant Parmesan

Serves 6 to 8 — ②

This dish involves a few steps but is well worth the time and effort.

2 pounds eggplant
Sea salt
1 tablespoon olive oil
1 onion, chopped
2-3 cloves garlic, to taste, minced or put through a press
3 pounds tomatoes, chopped
2 tablespoons tomato paste
1 tablespoon chopped fresh basil or 1 teaspoon dried basil
½ teaspoon thyme (or more, to taste)
Freshly ground black pepper, to taste
Pinch of cinnamon
2 eggs, beaten in a bowl
Olive oil for frying
1 pound mozzarella cheese, sliced thinly
4 ounces Parmesan cheese, grated
Fresh chopped parsley

1. Slice eggplant ½-inch thick. Arrange on plates and salt lightly. Weight with plates and let sit about 1 hour. Rinse and pat dry.

2. Meanwhile make a tomato sauce. Heat the tablespoon of olive oil in a heavy-bottomed saucepan and sauté onion and garlic over medium-low heat until onion is tender.

3. Add tomatoes and tomato paste, bring to a simmer, and simmer 30 minutes.

4. Add herbs, pepper, and cinnamon and simmer for another 15 minutes or so. Adjust seasonings.

5. Heat enough oil in a frying pan to coat the bottom. Dip eggplant slices in beaten egg and sauté on both sides until crisp and browned. Drain on paper towels.

6. Preheat oven to 350°F.

7. Oil a large baking dish or casserole. Spoon in a very thin layer of tomato

sauce and top with sautéed eggplant slices. Top with mozzarella slices, then a layer of tomato sauce, then a layer of Parmesan. Make one or two more layers in this order, ending with Parmesan.

8. Bake in preheated oven 40 minutes. Remove from heat, sprinkle on parsley, and serve.

Eggplant, Potatoes, Garlic, and Tofu Stewed in Brandy

Serves 6 to 8 ②

The vegetables here are stewed very slowly for 2 hours and absorb the perfume of the brandy. The eggplant falls apart and thickens the combination. It is a heavenly dish. You may add more water if it seems dry to you.

1 tablespoon butter or safflower oil
1 onion, sliced
½ pound tofu, diced
1 tablespoon soy sauce
1 teaspoon whole wheat flour
Cloves from 1 head garlic, peeled and left whole
1 pound eggplant, diced
1 pound boiling potatoes, diced
½ cup brandy
½ cup water or Vegetable Stock (page 60)
½ teaspoon *Vegex* or *Marmite*
Freshly ground black pepper, to taste
Fresh thyme for garnish

1. In a large, heavy-bottomed, lidded casserole heat butter or oil and brown onion over moderate heat.

2. Add tofu and soy sauce and sauté another 5 minutes. Add flour and stir together a minute or two, then add garlic and eggplant and a little more oil if necessary.

3. Sauté about 3 minutes to coat with oil. Add potatoes, brandy, water or stock, and *Vegex* or *Marmite* and bring to a simmer.

4. Reduce heat, place over very low heat, preferably on flameproof pad, cover, and simmer slowly 2 hours. Stir from time to time, and add more water or stock if necessary.

5. Add pepper, taste and add salt if you wish, and serve, garnishing with leaves of fresh thyme.

Curried Zucchini

Serves 4 to 6 ———————————— ①

---

1 tablespoon safflower or peanut oil

1 small onion, sliced

1 clove garlic, minced or put through a press

½ teaspoon grated fresh ginger

2 teaspoons curry powder (or more, to taste)

½ teaspoon ground cumin or crushed cumin seeds

2 pounds zucchini, sliced diagonally ¼-inch thick

2 tablespoons water or Vegetable Stock (page 60)

Sea salt and freshly ground black pepper, to taste

½ cup plain low-fat yogurt (optional)

Fresh chopped mint or coriander, for garnish

Chutney or raisins, for garnish

---

1. Heat oil in a frying pan and sauté onion and garlic until onion begins to soften — about 3 minutes.

2. Add ginger, curry powder, and cumin and sauté another 3 minutes.

3. Add zucchini, stir together for a minute or two, and add water or vegetable stock.

4. Cook, stirring from time to time, 15 minutes. Add salt and pepper to taste and adjust seasonings.

5. Remove from heat and stir in yogurt, if using.

6. Serve with grains, garnishing with chopped fresh mint or coriander and chutney or raisins.

Zucchini à la Provençale

Serves 4 to 6 ②

---

1 tablespoon olive oil

1½ pounds zucchini, sliced diagonally ¼-inch thick

1-2 cloves garlic, to taste, minced or put through a press

1 pound tomatoes, chopped

1 teaspoon chopped fresh basil, plus more for garnish

¼-½ teaspoon thyme, to taste

Sea salt and freshly ground black pepper, to taste

---

1. Heat olive oil in a wide, heavy-bottomed frying pan and sauté zucchini with garlic over medium heat 5 minutes.

2. Add tomatoes, basil, thyme, and salt and bring to a simmer. Cook over medium heat, stirring from time to time, 15 to 20 minutes.

3. Add freshly ground pepper to taste, adjust seasonings, and serve with a little more basil for garnish.

Garlic Mashed Potatoes

Serves 6 ③

---

6 large baking potatoes

Butter or oil

2 heads garlic, cloves separated and peeled

1 cup low-fat milk or plain yogurt

Sea salt and freshly ground black pepper, to taste

Paprika

Additional butter (optional)

---

1. Preheat oven to 425°F. Scrub potatoes, dry, and pierce in a couple of places with a sharp knife. Rub with a little oil or butter.

2. Wrap peeled garlic cloves in foil envelopes, drizzling with some oil or dotting with butter.

3. Place potatoes and garlic in oven and bake 45 minutes, or until tender. Remove from heat. Turn oven down to 350°F.

4. Remove garlic from foil, mash to a purée, and blend with milk or yogurt, salt, and freshly ground pepper to taste.

5. Holding potatoes with a towel or potholder, cut them open lengthwise down the middle. Remove flesh from skins and mash, using a ricer or potato masher. Blend in garlic-milk mixture and adjust seasonings.

6. Place back in potato skins and sprinkle with paprika. If you wish, place a pat of butter on each potato. Heat through 15 to 20 minutes.

Potato Gratin with Garlic

Serves 6

2 pounds boiling potatoes
6 cloves garlic, thinly sliced
2 tablespoons butter
Sea salt and freshly ground black pepper, to taste
4 ounces grated Gruyère cheese
1 cup boiling milk

1. Preheat oven to 425°F.

2. Wash potatoes and slice ½-inch thick. Place in a bowl of cold water as you do this. When they are all sliced, drain and dry in a towel.

3. Butter a 2-inch deep 10-inch flameproof gratin or baking dish. Layer half the potatoes and dot with half the garlic slices, half the butter, some salt and freshly ground pepper, and half the grated cheese. Repeat layers and pour on boiling milk.

4. Set over medium heat and bring to a simmer. Place in upper third of oven and bake for 30 minutes, or until milk has been absorbed and top is browned. Serve.

Cold Tomato and Pepper Casserole

Serves 4 to 6 ————————————————— ①

This dish is a bit watery, but the juices are delicious and should be spooned over each serving.

2 large sweet red peppers
1 large green pepper
2 tablespoons olive oil
1 small onion, sliced
2 cloves garlic, minced or put through a press
2 ounces chopped fresh parsley
2 ounces chopped fresh basil or 1 tablespoon dried basil
1 teaspoon thyme
Sea salt and freshly ground black pepper
2 pounds tomatoes, sliced
2 ounces freshly grated Parmesan cheese
2 tablespoons whole wheat bread crumbs

1. Preheat oven to 400°F. Brush peppers with some of the olive oil and place under broiler.

2. Cook under broiler about 5 minutes, or until skin blisters. Turn and continue to cook on all sides until peppers are thoroughly blistered. *

3. Remove from heat and wrap in a damp tea towel or place in a plastic bag.

4. Meanwhile heat 1 tablespoon of the oil and sauté onion and garlic over low heat until onion is tender. Set aside.

5. When peppers are cool enough to handle, peel under cold water. Cut in half and carefully discard seeds and membranes. Dry with paper towels and cut into 1-inch strips.

6. Combine herbs. Oil a 1½-quart baking dish with olive oil and cover with a third of the sliced tomatoes. Season with a little salt and pepper, and sprinkle with a third of the cheese and a third of the herb mixture.

7. Layer half the peppers, alternating red and green, over herbs, and repeat layers, ending with last third of tomatoes, onions and garlic, Parmesan, and herbs.

8. Sprinkle bread crumbs over the top, grind on some pepper, and drizzle on remaining tablespoon of oil.

9. Bake 20 minutes, remove from heat and let sit for 15 minutes. Refrigerate 2 hours and serve chilled.

Note: The peppers can also be roasted directly over a flame if you have a gas range. Turn on a burner and place a pepper over the flame. Turn at regular intervals until evenly charred. Remove from heat and wrap in a damp tea towel or a plastic bag.

Baked Whole Tomatoes
à la Provençale

Serves 4 to 6 ——————————①

4-6 firm, large ripe tomatoes
2 cloves garlic, minced
2 shallots, minced
2 tablespoons chopped fresh parsley
2 tablespoons chopped fresh basil, if available (Do not substitute dried.)
½ teaspoon thyme
¼ teaspoon crushed rosemary
Sea salt and freshly ground black pepper
3 tablespoons whole wheat bread crumbs
Olive oil

1. Preheat oven to 400°F.

2. Cut tomatoes across the top, about ½-inch down from stem. Gently scoop out seeds and place upside-down on a rack for 10 minutes.

3. Mix together shallots, garlic, and herbs. Place tomatoes cut side up on an oiled baking sheet or in an oiled baking pan.

4. Lightly salt and pepper, and sprinkle with herbs and garlic mixture, then with bread crumbs.

5. Drizzle on a little olive oil and bake 10 minutes. They should be cooked through but still hold their shape. Remove from heat and serve.

Illustrated opposite page 80.

Sautéed Spinach with Garlic
Serves 6 ———————————————— ②

There are two ways to do this dish. The second method yields a more subtly flavored dish, as the garlic is removed from the oil before the spinach is added.

---

2 pounds spinach

2 tablespoons olive oil

2 large cloves garlic

Sea salt and freshly ground black pepper

---

1. Wash spinach and remove stems. Heat a dry non-aluminum frying pan and sauté spinach in its own liquid until it wilts. Remove from heat, refresh under cold water, and squeeze out moisture.

Method 1:
2. Mince garlic or put through a press. Heat olive oil in the same frying pan and add garlic. Sauté gently about 2 minutes and add spinach.

3. Sauté about 2 to 3 minutes, stirring, until coated with garlicky oil. Add salt and pepper to taste and serve.

Method 2:
2. Cut cloves of garlic in half. Heat oil and sauté garlic for 3 minutes, or until it begins to turn color.

3. Remove garlic from pan and add spinach.

4. Sauté about 2 to 3 minutes, stirring, until spinach is well coated in oil. Season to taste and serve.

Green Beans and Red Peppers Sautéed with Garlic

Serves 4 to 6 ———————————

1 pound green beans, trimmed
1 tablespoon olive oil
1 clove garlic, minced or put through a press
1½ sweet red peppers, seeds and membranes removed, cut in thin lengthwise strips

1. Trim beans, and meanwhile bring a large pot of water to a rolling boil. Add some salt, then dump in beans.
2. As soon as water comes back to a rolling boil count 1 minute, then drain beans and rinse with cold water. (Alternatively, beans can be steamed 5 minutes.)
3. Heat olive oil in a frying pan and add garlic and red peppers. Sauté 5 minutes, or until peppers are tender, and add beans.
4. Cook, tossing, until heated through. Place mixture in a mound on a big serving dish or platter and serve.

Illustrated opposite page 112.

Green Beans à la Provençale

Serves 6 ——————————— ②

1½ pounds green beans, trimmed
1 tablespoon olive oil
1 pound ripe tomatoes, chopped
2 cloves garlic, minced or put through a press
½ teaspoon thyme
1 tablespoon chopped fresh basil or 1 teaspoon dried
Sea salt and freshly ground black pepper, to taste

1. Steam beans 5 to 10 minutes and refresh under cold water.
2. Heat oil in a large saucepan and add tomatoes and garlic. Simmer over medium-high heat 10 minutes.
3. Add beans, herbs, and salt and pepper to taste, cover, reduce heat to medium-low, and cook another 10 minutes. Stir from time to time.
4. Remove from heat and serve.

Green Beans Amandine
Serves 4

---

1 pound tender green beans, trimmed

2 tablespoons butter

2 ounces flaked almonds

1 clove garlic, minced or put through a press

Sea salt and freshly ground black pepper, to taste

---

1. Steam beans 10 minutes. Refresh under cold water.
2. Heat butter and sauté almonds with garlic until they begin to turn color.
3. Add beans and continue to sauté another 3 minutes or so, or until completely heated through. Add salt and freshly ground pepper to taste, and serve.

Leeks à la Niçoise
Serves 4 to 6 ——————————②

---
2 pounds leeks, white part only, thoroughly cleaned
---
2 tablespoons olive oil
---
1 tablespoon vinegar
---
2 cloves garlic, minced or put through a press
---
1 pound tomatoes

½ teaspoon thyme

Sea salt and freshly ground black pepper, to taste

Pinch of cayenne
---
1 tablespoon fresh chopped parsley
---

1. Clean leeks by trimming off root end and green stalk, then slitting down center and running under cold water until all the sand and grit is washed away.

2. Heat oil in a frying pan or saucepan and lay leeks in it side by side. Cook 2 minutes and turn over. Sprinkle with a little salt, cook a minute, then turn down heat.

3. Add 1 tablespoon of water and one tablespoon of vinegar, cover the pan, and cook 10 minutes, or a little longer if very large. The root end should be tender. Remove from pan and place in a serving dish in a warm oven.

4. Keep flame moderate and add garlic to frying pan. Cook a minute and add tomatoes.

5. Cook 10 minutes, stirring occasionally, and add thyme, salt, and pepper. Cook another 5 minutes, add a pinch of cayenne and the parsley, and pour over leeks. Serve hot, or cool and chill.

Opposite: Green Beans and Red Pepper Sautéed with Garlic (page 110) and Cauliflower Vinaigrette with Peas (page 187).

Turnips with Vinegar and Garlic

Serves 4 to 6

2 pounds turnips

2 tablespoons olive oil

2-3 cloves garlic, puréed or put through a press

2 tablespoons red wine vinegar

Sea salt and freshly ground black pepper, to taste

1. Choose young, small, tender turnips. Peel, and if they are large cut in half. Place in a steamer above boiling water, cover, and steam 10 minutes. Refresh under cold water and cut into quarters.

2. Heat olive oil in a heavy-bottomed frying pan and add turnips. Stew in olive oil over medium-low heat 5 to 10 minutes.

3. Combine garlic and vinegar and stir into turnips. Turn heat to medium and cook until vinegar is reduced and glazes turnips — about 5 minutes. Add salt and freshly ground pepper to taste, and serve.

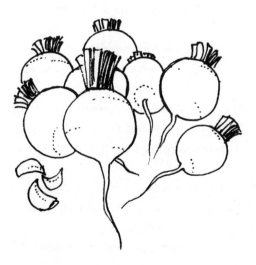

Sautéed Tofu and Vegetables

Serves 6 to 8 ①

For the tofu:

¾ pound tofu, diced

½ cup soy sauce

½ cup water

1 clove garlic, crushed

1 teaspoon minced or grated fresh ginger

½ teaspoon cinnamon

¼ teaspoon ground allspice

¼ teaspoon crushed anise

⅛ teaspoon ground cloves

For the sauce:

½ cup strained marinade from the tofu

1 cup Vegetable Stock (page 60) or bouillon

2 tablespoons dry sherry

1 teaspoon honey

1 teaspoon vinegar

1 tablespoon cornstarch (more, if necessary)

For the vegetables:

2 tablespoons safflower, peanut, or sesame oil

1 clove garlic, minced or put through a press

1 teaspoon minced or grated fresh ginger

1 onion, sliced thinly

4 ounces sliced fresh mushrooms

1 stick celery, sliced

2 ounces walnuts

4 ounces trimmed snow peas

½ pound mung bean sprouts

1. Combine all ingredients for tofu in a saucepan and simmer 10 minutes. Drain and retain marinade.

2. Mix together ingredients for sauce and set aside.

3. Heat a wok or a large frying pan over a high flame and add oil. Stir-fry garlic, ginger, and onion 2 minutes, or until onion is translucent.

4. Remove from pan, place in a bowl, and add to pan mushrooms and tofu. Stir-fry 3 minutes and add celery, walnuts, and snow peas. Stir-fry 1 more minute, or until peas are bright green.

5. Return other ingredients to wok and add bean sprouts. Toss together and pour in sauce. Cook, stirring, until sauce glazes vegetables.

6. If sauce doesn't thicken within a couple of minutes, add another teaspoon of cornstarch dissolved in a little water. Serve over grains or noodles.

Sautéed Cabbage and Onions with Garlic

Serves 4 ──────────────── ②

2 tablespoons safflower or vegetable oil
1 large onion, cut in half and sliced in thin strips
2 cloves garlic, minced or put through a press
1 tablespoon soy sauce
1 tablespoon sesame seeds
1 pound shredded red or white cabbage

1. Heat oil in a large, heavy-bottomed frying pan or wok. Add onion and sauté over medium heat until it begins to brown.

2. Add garlic and continue to sauté another 5 minutes.

3. Add soy sauce, sesame seeds, and cabbage and stir-fry 5 to 10 minutes over medium-high heat, adding more oil if necessary. Serve with grains.

Turnips with Parsley and Bread Crumbs

Serves 4 to 6

---

2 pounds turnips

1 tablespoon olive oil

1 clove garlic, minced or put through a press

4 tablespoons whole wheat bread crumbs

3 tablespoons chopped fresh parsley

Sea salt and freshly ground black pepper, to taste

---

1. Try to find small, young turnips. Peel, cut in half if large, place in a steamer above boiling water, cover, and steam 10 minutes. Drain and refresh under cold water. Cut into quarters.

2. Heat olive oil in a frying pan and sauté garlic until golden — about 1 minute.

3. Add turnips and turn heat to low. Cover and cook about 10 minutes, shaking pan occasionally to make sure they don't stick.

4. Add bread crumbs and parsley and continue to cook until oil is absorbed and bread crumbs crisp. Season to taste with salt and freshly ground pepper.

CHAPTER VI

GRAINS, LEGUMES, AND PASTA

When I told friends that I was working on a book of garlic recipes, pasta was always the first thing that came to their minds, especially if they were familiar with Fettuccine con Aglio e Olio (page 136)-pasta with oil and garlic. It's true that one could fill a book with recipes for different combinations of pasta and redolent sauces pungent with garlic and other herbs. But along with pasta go grains and legumes, with as many marvelous variations. I would never think of cooking dried beans without garlic, for it is an abundance of this ingredient that is the key to a great pot of beans. Cooking whole cloves of garlic along with grains like rice or millet is an ingenious way to dress up a simple dish, a trick I learned from my landlady in Provence. But there are many more elaborate combinations, all of which prove how delicious and varied grains and legumes can be.

Most of the recipes in this chapter make substantial main dishes and go well with green salads and vegetable side dishes.

Brown Rice and Garlic
Serves 6 ——————(2)

If you wish, soak the rice for an hour in 3 times its volume of water. This optional step renders the grains a little more tender.

½ pound raw brown rice, washed

1 tablespoon safflower oil

6 cloves garlic, lightly crushed, skins removed

2 cups water

½ teaspoon sea salt (or to taste)

Soy sauce or butter

---

1. Heat oil in a heavy-bottomed saucepan and sauté garlic 2 minutes, or until it begins to turn color.

2. Add rice and sauté a minute or two, until thoroughly coated with oil. Add water and bring to a boil. Add salt, reduce heat, and cover.

3. Simmer 35 minutes and check to see if water has been absorbed. If not, simmer another 10 minutes without disturbing. If so, add a further 4 tablespoons boiling water and simmer, covered, for another 5 to 10 minutes.

4. Let sit, covered, 10 minutes off the heat, then fluff and serve with soy sauce or a little butter.

Note: Feel free to use more or less garlic here, according to your taste. Also, millet could be substituted for the rice. If so, before heating the oil in the pan, toast the millet over dry heat just until it begins to smell fragrant, and remove from the heat.

Brown Rice Risotto with Broccoli

Serves 6

3 cups Vegetable or Garlic Broth (page 60), or more if needed
½ teaspoon *Vegex* or *Marmite*
1 tablespoon safflower oil
¼ onion, minced
1 clove garlic, minced or put through a press
½ pound brown rice, washed
½ cup dry white wine
½ pound broccoli florets
¼-½ teaspoon thyme, to taste
2 ounces freshly grated Parmesan cheese
Sea salt and freshly ground black pepper, to taste
1 egg, beaten with 4 tablespoons hot broth (optional)

1. Have Vegetable Stock or Garlic Broth simmering in a saucepan. Stir in *Vegex* or *Marmite*.

2. Heat safflower oil in a large, heavy-bottomed saucepan and sauté onion and garlic 3 minutes over medium heat.

3. Add rice and continue to sauté, stirring, until thoroughly coated with oil (another 2 to 3 minutes).

4. Add white wine and cook, stirring, over medium heat, until wine is just about absorbed. Pour in simmering stock, bring to a boil, reduce heat, cover, and simmer 30 minutes.

5. Add broccoli and thyme and more liquid if necessary, cover, and cook another 5 to 10 minutes. There should still be some broth.

6. Stir in Parmesan, add salt and freshly ground pepper to taste, and the optional egg beaten with stock; remove from heat and serve.

Risotto al Limone
——————— Serves 6 ——————— ①

---

3 cups simmering Vegetable Stock or Garlic Broth (page 60)

1 tablespoon safflower oil

1-2 cloves garlic, to taste, minced or put through a press

¼ onion, finely chopped

½ pound brown rice, washed

½ cup dry white wine

4 ounces freshly grated Parmesan

Sea salt and freshly ground black pepper, to taste

Juice of 1 lemon

Finely grated rind of ½ lemon

1 egg yolk

2 tablespoons Vegetable Stock or Garlic Broth (page 60)

1. Have Vegetable Stock or Garlic Broth simmering in a saucepan.

2. In a large, heavy-bottomed saucepan heat oil and sauté garlic and onion about 2 minutes over medium heat.

3. Add rice and continue to sauté about 3 minutes, or until thoroughly coated with oil.

4. Add white wine and cook, stirring, over medium heat, until wine is just about absorbed. Add simmering stock, bring to a boil, cover, reduce heat, and simmer 30 minutes.

5. Check to see that there is still some broth, and add a little bit if necessary.

6. Cook another 5 minutes, stir in Parmesan, and continue to cook another couple of minutes, stirring. There should still be some broth. Add salt and freshly ground pepper to taste and remove from heat.

7. Beat together lemon juice and rind, egg yolk, and the 2 tablespoons broth, and stir into rice. Serve at once.

Brown Rice Risotto with Mushrooms

Serves 6 ──────────── ②

3 cups Vegetable Stock or Garlic Broth (page 60), or more if needed
½ teaspoon *Vegex* or *Marmite*
2 tablespoons butter, safflower oil or olive oil, or a combination
2 shallots, minced
2 cloves garlic, minced or put through a press
½ pound mushrooms, cleaned, trimmed, and sliced fairly thin
½ pound raw brown rice, washed
½ cup dry white wine
½ teaspoon thyme
2 tablespoons chopped fresh parsley
2 ounces freshly grated Parmesan cheese
Sea salt and freshly ground black pepper, to taste
1 egg, beaten with 4 tablespoons hot broth (optional)

1. Combine *Vegex* or *Marmite* and stock and bring to a simmer in a saucepan.

2. In another heavy-bottomed saucepan or casserole heat butter or oil and sauté shallots and garlic 3 minutes.

3. Add mushrooms and sauté another 3 minutes.

4. Add rice and continue to sauté, stirring over medium heat, until rice is thoroughly coated with oil or butter, another 2 to 3 minutes.

5. Add thyme and white wine and continue stirring over medium heat until wine is just about absorbed.

6. Stir in simmering stock, bring to a boil, reduce heat, and cover. Simmer 30 minutes and check to see if there is still enough broth. Add a little more if necessary.

7. Cover and cook another 5 to 10 minutes, or until rice is *al dente*. There should still be some broth.

8. Add parsley, Parmesan, salt and pepper to taste, and the optional egg. Mix together well and serve.

Curried Rice with Lentils and Garlic

Serves 6 ———————————————②

---

1 tablespoon safflower oil, peanut oil, or butter

4 cloves garlic, sliced

1 small onion, chopped

½-inch piece of fresh ginger, minced or grated

½ teaspoon turmeric

½ teaspoon crushed cumin seeds

¼ teaspoon ground allspice

2 teaspoons curry powder (or more, to taste)

6 ounces raw brown rice, washed

6 ounces lentils, washed and picked over

3 cups water

Sea salt, to taste

Plain yogurt and raisins for garnish

---

1. Heat oil in a large heavy-bottomed lidded saucepan and sauté garlic, onion, and ginger until golden. Add spices and sauté another few minutes.

2. Add rice and lentils and sauté a few minutes to coat with oil, then add water. Bring to a boil, add salt to taste, reduce heat, cover, and simmer 35 minutes.

3. Check for water, pour in another 4 tablespoons boiling water if all the water has been absorbed, cover, and simmer another 10 minutes.

4. Remove from heat, let sit 10 to 15 minutes, and serve topped with yogurt and raisins.

Polenta with Sautéed Mushrooms

Serves 6 to 8

1 recipe Sautéed Mushrooms, page 94

½ pound coarse-grained cornmeal or packaged polenta

1½-2 teaspoons sea salt

6 cups water (or more for a creamier polenta)

1. Make Sautéed Mushrooms and set aside.

2. Bring water to a rolling boil in a large, heavy-bottomed soup pot or saucepan. Add salt and turn heat to medium-low so that water is just simmering.

3. Add cornmeal in a very slow stream, stirring all the while with a long-handled wooden spoon. You should be able to see the separate grains as you pour. One way to do this is to take up handfuls of the polenta and let it slip through your fingers.

4. Once all the polenta has been added, continue to stir steadily 15 to 20 minutes, or until mixture is stiff and tears away from sides of the pot as you stir.

5. If you want a creamier polenta, add an extra cup of water and don't stir quite as long. When the polenta is cooked, transfer it to a large platter, make a shallow depression in the middle, and pour on the mushrooms. Serve at once.

Barley with Mushrooms and Garlic

Serves 6 ②

---

3 cups Vegetable Stock or Garlic Stock (page 60)

1 tablespoon safflower oil or butter, more as needed

1 onion, chopped

1 pound mushrooms, cleaned, stems trimmed and sliced

2-4 cloves garlic, minced (to taste)

1 tablespoon soy sauce

2 tablespoons dry white wine

½ teaspoon thyme

½ pound barley, washed

Sea salt and freshly ground black pepper, to taste

---

1. Bring broth to a boil in a saucepan.

2. Preheat oven to 350°F.

3. Heat butter or oil in a large, lidded casserole and sauté onion until tender. Add mushrooms and garlic and sauté until mushrooms begin to release some of their liquid — about 2 to 3 minutes.

4. Add soy sauce, white wine, and thyme and continue to sauté another 3 minutes.

5. Stir in barley and sauté 1 minute, then pour in broth and bring to a second boil. Add a little salt and pepper, cover, and place in preheated oven.

6. Bake 30 to 40 minutes, or until barley is tender. Check liquid from time to time and add more if necessary.

Curried Millet with Garlic
Serves 4 ——————————————— ②

6 ounces millet
1 tablespoon safflower or peanut oil
½ teaspoon cumin seeds
1 small onion, chopped
2 cloves garlic, sliced thin
½-inch piece fresh ginger, minced or grated
½ teaspoon turmeric
1½ teaspoons curry powder
1½ cups water
Sea salt, to taste

1. Roast millet in a dry frying pan until it begins to smell toasted. Set aside.

2. Heat oil in a heavy-bottomed saucepan and add cumin seeds, onion, and garlic.

3. Sauté until onion is tender and add ginger, turmeric, and curry powder.

4. Sauté another minute and add millet. Stir together and pour in water.

5. Bring to a boil, add salt, reduce heat, cover, and simmer for 35 minutes. Check to see if water has been absorbed, and if it has, add 4 tablespoons boiling water and cook, undisturbed, another 10 minutes.

6. Remove from heat and let sit for 15 minutes, covered, before serving.

Spiced Bulgur Pilaf with Nuts and Raisins

Serves 4 to 6

½ pound bulgur
3 tablespoons safflower, peanut, or vegetable oil
2 tablespoons slivered almonds
2 tablespoons halved cashews
2 tablespoons pine nuts
5 tablespoons sultanas
½ teaspoon cumin seeds
½ teaspoon crushed cardamom seeds
1 small onion, sliced very thin
1 clove garlic, minced
1-inch piece fresh ginger, peeled and grated or minced
3 cups water
Sea salt, to taste
Additional raisins and pine nuts or sunflower seeds, for garnish

1. Heat oil in a heavy-bottomed saucepan or lidded frying pan or wok and sauté almonds until they begin to brown. Remove from oil and transfer to a bowl. Repeat the process with cashews and pine nuts.

2. Add raisins, and as soon as they puff up remove from heat.

3. Add cumin, onion, garlic, and ginger and sauté until onion is tender.

4. Add bulgur and stir together, then stir in nuts and raisins and water. Bring to a boil, add salt to taste, cover, reduce heat, and simmer 15 minutes, or until water is absorbed and bulgur tender.

5. Remove from heat and let sit 15 minutes. Serve garnished with raisins and sunflower seeds or pine nuts, and serve yogurt on the side.

Bulgur and Chickpeas with Tomatoes and Garlic

Serves 6 ——————————————②

1 tablespoon safflower or olive oil
1 onion, finely chopped
2 cloves garlic, minced
½-¾ pound ripe tomatoes, peeled and minced
4 ounces raw chickpeas, cooked (reserve cooking liquid)
Sea salt, to taste
½ teaspoon thyme
2 tablespoons minced fresh parsley
6 ounces bulgur
2 cups water or cooking liquid from the chickpeas
Freshly ground black pepper

1. Heat oil in a large, heavy-bottomed casserole or saucepan over a medium flame and sauté onion and garlic until onion is tender.

2. Add tomatoes and cook another 5 minutes.

3. Add cooked chickpeas and salt to taste and cook, stirring occasionally, about 10 minutes.

4. Add herbs, bulgur and water or broth from chickpeas, bring to a simmer, cover, and simmer over very low heat 15 to 20 minutes, or until liquid is absorbed and bulgur tender.

5. Remove from heat, remove lid, cover with a tea towel and return lid to the pot. Let sit 15 minutes. Add pepper to taste, adjust salt, and serve. This can be frozen.

Slow Cooked Beans and Rice

Serves 6 ②

This is one of the most exquisite bean dishes I know of, and it's so simple. The extremely slow cooking of the beans, with all the garlic, yields a rich, thick broth, and the beans are very soft and digestible.

---

1 pound red or black beans, washed and picked over

1 large onion, chopped

6 large cloves garlic, minced

8 cups water

Sea salt and freshly ground black pepper, to taste

6 ounces brown rice, cooked

---

1. Heat oven on its lowest setting.

2. Combine beans, onion, garlic, and water in a large, lidded, ovenproof casserole and place in oven. Do not add salt.

3. Cook in slow oven overnight, or all day, 6 to 10 hours.

4. Check liquid after 6 or 7 hours and add more if necessary.

5. When beans are tender and liquid is thick and soupy, add salt to taste, and stir in cooked brown rice and some pepper.

Opposite: Spaghettini with Fresh Peas and Herb Butter (page 138) and Pasta with Spicy Broccoli (page 137).

White Beans à la Provençale

Serves 6 ②

---

1 pound white beans, washed and picked over

1 tablespoon olive oil

1 onion, chopped

2 cloves garlic, minced or put through a press

5 cups water

1 bay leaf

Sea salt, to taste

1 additional tablespoon olive oil

1-2 additional cloves garlic, minced or put through a press

1 pound tomatoes, peeled and chopped

Fresh or dried thyme, to taste

Fresh or dried basil, to taste

Freshly ground black pepper, to taste

1. Soak beans in three times their volume water overnight or for several hours.

2. In a large, heavy-bottomed saucepan or casserole heat oil and sauté 1 onion and 2 cloves garlic until onion is tender.

3. Drain beans and add them, along with fresh water and bay leaf.

4. Bring to a boil, reduce heat, cover, and simmer 1 hour, or until tender. Add salt to taste. Remove bay leaf, drain, and retain cooking liquid.

5. Heat additional olive oil in a wide, heavy-bottomed frying pan or casserole and sauté extra garlic 1 minute. Add tomatoes and herbs, salt to taste, and simmer 5 minutes.

6. Add beans, along with a cup of their cooking liquid, and continue to simmer, covered, 15 minutes. Adjust seasonings and serve.

Potaje de Garbanzos (Tomato & Chickpea Stew)

Serves 6 ②

This is based on a Spanish dish that is served as a thick soup. Serve it that way or as a side or main dish. It is a meal in itself, with whole grain bread and a salad.

1 tablespoon olive oil
1 large onion, chopped
4 large cloves garlic, minced
1 teaspoon paprika (or more, to taste)
1 pound ripe tomatoes (fresh or canned), peeled, seeded, and chopped
1 bay leaf
4 tablespoons tomato paste
2 medium boiling potatoes, diced
1 teaspoon thyme
1 teaspoon oregano
2 cups broth from the beans
1 pound chickpeas, cooked (reserve the broth)
Sea salt and freshly ground black pepper, to taste

1. In a heavy-bottomed saucepan or casserole heat olive oil and add onion and garlic. Sauté until onion is tender, and add paprika.
2. Stir a minute, and add tomatoes, bay leaf, and tomato paste. Simmer together over medium heat 10 minutes.
3. Add potatoes, thyme, oregano, broth from beans, chickpeas, and salt to taste.
4. Bring to a boil, reduce heat, cover, and simmer 30 minutes, or until potatoes are tender. Stir from time to time. Add plenty of ground pepper and adjust seasonings. Serve.

Lentils with Herb Butter

Serves 6 — ②

1 pound lentils
1 small onion, chopped
2 cloves garlic, minced or put through a press
1 bay leaf
Sea salt, to taste
Freshly ground black pepper
4 tablespoons Herb Butter (page 22)

1. Soak lentils in 3 times their volume of water 1 hour and drain.

2. Combine lentils, onion, garlic, and bay leaf in a large saucepan and add water to cover by 2 inches. Bring to a boil, add salt to taste, reduce heat, cover, and simmer 45 minutes, or until lentils are tender. Pour off stock, if much remains, stir in plenty of black pepper, and stir in Herb Butter. Serve.

Succotash with Tomatoes and Garlic

Serves 6 to 8 ─────────────── ③

Succotash is a native American dish that is based on the combination of corn and beans. It has evolved into a dish that is usually made with lima beans though other beans could be substituted.

1 tablespoon safflower oil
1 onion, chopped
6-8 cloves garlic, minced or put through a press
1 pound dried lima beans, washed, picked over, and soaked overnight
6 cups water
Sea salt, to taste
1 tablespoon olive oil
6 additional cloves garlic
1 teaspoon rosemary
1 teaspoon thyme
⅔ cup red wine
2 pounds ripe tomatoes, peeled and coarsely chopped or same amount canned tomatoes with their liquid, chopped
6 ounces tomato paste if using fresh tomatoes
3 cups liquid from the beans
Kernels from 2-3 ears corn
Generous amount of freshly ground black pepper
2 tablespoons chopped fresh parsley
3 ounces freshly grated Parmesan cheese (optional)

1. First cook beans. In a heavy-bottomed saucepan or bean pot heat safflower oil and sauté onion and the first 6-8 cloves of garlic until onion is tender.

2. Add beans and water, bring to a boil, cover, and reduce heat. Cook 1 to 2 hours, or until tender but not mushy. Add salt to taste.

3. Remove from heat, drain, and reserve liquid. Save what you don't use in the succotash for soups.

4. Heat olive oil in your bean pot and add remaining garlic and rosemary and thyme. Sauté a few minutes over low heat, or until garlic begins to turn gold.

5. Add red wine, tomatoes, tomato paste if you are using it, and simmer over low heat 20 minutes, stirring often. Add salt to taste.

6. Add lima beans, 3 cups of their liquid, and corn. Continue to simmer 10 to 15 minutes, stirring from time to time.

7. Grind in a generous amount of black pepper and adjust seasonings. Ladle into bowls and top with parsley and optional Parmesan. Serve hot.

Pasta and Chickpeas

Serves 6 to 8

1 pound chickpeas, soaked
6 cups water
1 onion, chopped
4 large cloves garlic, minced or put through a press
3 tablespoons olive oil
2 pounds ripe tomatoes or the equivalent canned, chopped
1 teaspoon fresh basil, chopped, or ½ teaspoonful dried
½ teaspoon oregano
½-1 teaspoon crushed rosemary, to taste
Sea salt and freshly ground black pepper, to taste
1 small dried hot red pepper
6 ounces spiral pasta or macaroni
3 tablespoons fresh chopped parsley
2 ounces freshly grated Parmesan cheese

1. Drain soaked beans. Combine with water in a large saucepan, bring to a boil, reduce heat, and cook 2 hours, or until soft. Add salt to taste. Do not drain.

2. Meanwhile make a tomato sauce. Heat 1 tablespoon of olive oil in a heavy-bottomed saucepan or large frying pan and add onion and 2 cloves of garlic.

3. Cook gently until onion is tender and add tomatoes. Stir together and simmer, uncovered, ½ hour, stirring occasionally.

4. Add oregano, basil, salt, and pepper and continue to cook 15 minutes. Add to beans and mix well.

5. Heat remaining olive oil and sauté garlic and hot pepper over low heat until garlic begins to turn gold. Add to beans along with rosemary.

6. Let everything simmer together about 10 minutes. Make sure chickpeas are covered by at least 1 inch of liquid, and if they are not add a little more water. Taste and adjust seasonings.

7. Make sure chickpeas are simmering and stir in pasta. Cook until *al dente*. Stir in parsley and serve, passing Parmesan on the side.

Lasagne
Serves 6 to 8 ——————————②

4 cups Rich Tomato Sauce (page 162)
12 to 15 sheets lasagne, either spinach or whole wheat
1 pound ricotta cheese
2 eggs, beaten
2 small shallots, minced
1 clove garlic, puréed or put through a press
Freshly grated nutmeg
Freshly ground black pepper, to taste
1 pound mozzarella cheese, sliced
5 ounces freshly grated Parmesan cheese
1 ounce whole wheat breadcrumbs
Fresh chopped parsley, for garnish

1. First make Tomato Sauce, and set aside (can be done a day or two in advance).

2. Bring a large pot of water to a boil, add salt and a little oil and lasagne. Cook *al dente*, drain, and rinse in cold water. Toss with a little olive oil and set aside.

3. Preheat oven to 375°F. Oil a large wide gratin or baking dish.

4. Sauté shallots and garlic in 1 tablespoon oil until tender — about 2 minutes.

5. Mix together ricotta cheese, eggs, shallots, garlic, nutmeg to taste, and freshly ground pepper.

6. Spoon a thin layer of Tomato Sauce over bottom of baking dish. Over this lay three to four sheets of lasagne. Top with a third of the ricotta mixture, then a third of the sliced mozzarella, a third of the Tomato Sauce, a third of the Parmesan, and a third of the bread crumbs. Repeat layers — noodles, ricotta, mozzarella, Tomato Sauce, Parmesan, and bread crumbs — twice more.

7. Dot top layer of bread crumbs with butter, if you wish, and bake in preheated oven 30 minutes, or until bubbling.

8. Remove from heat, let sit a few minutes, and serve garnished with fresh chopped parsley.

Fettuccine Con Aglio e Olio

Serves 6 ③

This classic Italian way of preparing pasta, simply with oil and garlic, belongs in any collection of garlic recipes.

6 tablespoons olive oil
3 cloves garlic, finely minced
1 tablespoon sea salt
1 tablespoon oil
1 pound whole wheat or spinach fettuccine
3 ounces freshly grated Parmesan cheese
¾ ounce fresh minced parsley

1. Bring a large pot of water to a boil. Meanwhile heat olive oil with garlic in it in a small pan over very low heat. The garlic should simmer slowly and never brown.

2. When garlic is golden, remove from heat. This should coincide with water beginning to boil.

3. Add a tablespoon of salt to water, plus a tablespoon of cooking oil, and drop in pasta. Cook *al dente* and transfer to a warm serving dish with a slotted spoon or drain in a colander.

4. Toss at once with oil and garlic mixture, cheese, and parsley, and serve.

Pasta with Spicy Broccoli
Serves 6 ②

2 pounds broccoli, broken into florets
1 tablespoon olive oil
2 large cloves garlic, minced
1 small hot dried pepper, minced
1½ pounds tomatoes, sliced
2 tablespoons pine nuts, toasted
Sea salt, to taste
1 tablespoon vegetable oil
1 pound whole wheat spiral-shaped pasta or macaroni
3 ounces freshly grated Parmesan cheese (optional)

1. Steam broccoli florets 10 minutes and refresh under cold water. Begin heating water for pasta in a large pot.

2. In a wide, heavy-bottomed frying pan heat oil and sauté garlic and hot pepper about 1 minute, then add tomatoes and cook over medium-high heat 10 minutes.

3. Add toasted pine nuts and salt to taste, and stir in broccoli. Keep over a low flame while you cook pasta.

4. When water comes to a rolling boil, add salt, a tablespoon of oil, and pasta.

5. Cook *al dente*, drain, and toss immediately in a warm serving dish with tomato-broccoli sauce. Serve, and pass Parmesan in a separate bowl.

Illustrated opposite page 128.

Spaghetti with Fresh Peas and Herb Butter

Serves 6 ——————(1)

1 pound fresh peas in their pods, shelled
4 ounces butter, softened
½ ounce fresh chopped basil
½ ounce fresh chopped parsley
1 clove garlic, puréed or put through a press
3 tablespoons fresh minced chives
Sea salt
1 pound very thin spaghetti (spaghettini or fusilli)

1. Bring a large pot of water to a boil.

2. Meanwhile steam peas 10 minutes, or until tender but still bright green, and drain.

3. Chop herbs and blend into butter along with garlic. Add a little salt if you wish.

4. When water comes to a rolling boil, add a generous amount of salt, a spoonful of oil, and pasta. Cook *al dente*, drain, and toss immediately in a warm serving dish with peas and herb butter. Serve at once.

Illustrated opposite page 128.

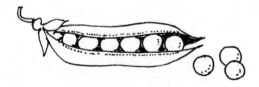

Baked Macaroni with Tomatoes and Cheese

Serves 6 — ②

---

1 recipe Quick, Light Tomato Sauce (page 162)

½ pound Cheddar cheese, grated

4 ounces freshly grated Parmesan cheese

Freshly ground black pepper

Sea salt

1 tablespoon oil

¾ pound elbow macaroni or flat noodles

2 tablespoons olive oil

1½ ounces whole wheat bread crumbs

1 tablespoon butter

---

1. Mix together grated cheeses and toss with ground pepper.

2. Bring a large pot of water to a boil, add salt and a spoonful of oil, and cook pasta slightly less than *al dente*, as it will cook further in the oven. Drain and toss with olive oil.

3. Preheat oven to 375°F and butter a large, deep baking dish.

4. Spoon a third of the Tomato Sauce over bottom of baking dish and top with a third of the noodles, then a third of the cheese. Repeat layers and top with bread crumbs. Dot with butter.

5. Bake, uncovered, 20 to 30 minutes, or until top browns and casserole is bubbling. Serve at once.

Soybean "Ground Beef"

Serves 6 ———————————— ②

Although I normally avoid anything that calls itself a "meat substitute," I can think of no better name for this preparation, for it can be used to replace ground beef in so many dishes, like spaghetti sauce, hamburgers, and casseroles. It is savory and good, and I have fooled many a meat eater with it.

For the basic "ground soybeans:"
½ pound dried soybeans
3 cups water
1 teaspoon sea salt
1 small onion

1. Soak soybeans overnight in water. In the morning grind them, a cup at a time, in a blender with onion, adding enough water to cover; you can use the soaking water.

2. Place ground soybeans in a very large saucepan, at least twice their volume. Add enough water to cover by 2 inches, and bring mixture slowly to a boil.

3. Add salt, reduce heat, and cover. Simmer 1 to 1½ hours, or until the liquid is absorbed. (A thin layer may stick to the bottom of the pan, but it will come off easily with soaking.)

For the "ground beef"
1 onion, minced
2 large cloves garlic, minced or put through a press
1 tablespoon safflower oil
2 vegetable bouillon cubes
1 cup tomato juice
1 tablespoon vegetarian Worcestershire sauce
1-2 tablespoons soy sauce, to taste
The cooked ground soybeans
½ teaspoon thyme
½ teaspoon sage
½ teaspoon paprika

1. In a large, heavy-bottomed frying pan, sauté onion and garlic in oil until tender.

2. Add bouillon cubes and mash with the back of a spoon, then add tomato juice, Worcestershire sauce and soy sauce, and cook together a few minutes over medium heat.

3. Add soybeans and herbs. Stir together and cook, uncovered, over a medium flame until almost dry — about 40 minutes. Stir from time to time to prevent sticking. Remove from heat. This freezes well.

Fettuccine with Pesto

Serves 6

Sea salt

1 tablespoon olive oil

1 pound whole wheat or spinach fettuccine

2 tablespoons hot water from the pasta

1 recipe Pesto (page 167)

2 tablespoons butter

2 tablespoons roasted pine nuts, for garnish

---

1. Bring a large pot of water to a rolling boil, add a generous amount of salt, and a spoonful of oil. Add pasta and cook *al dente*.

2. Add 2 tablespoons of cooking water to pesto, drain pasta, and transfer to a warm serving dish.

3. Toss with butter and serve, topping each serving with a generous helping of pesto and a sprinkling of pine nuts.

CHAPTER VII

EGGS, CHEESE, AND PIES

I remember eating some of the best scrambled eggs I'd ever tasted late one night after working all day and then going to the grocery store and coming home with a large bulb of elephant garlic. A friend who loved garlic even more than I do — a garlic fanatic — grabbed the great young bulb, cut up two or three huge cloves into thin slivers, and scrambled them into eggs. I slept extremely well after that delicious repast and never forgot the dish.

Garlic Scrambled Eggs (page 144) is the simplest of marriages. Beyond that, vegetable and garlic combinations make great fillings for omelettes or quiches, and bases for pastry shells. In fact these are great vehicles for leftovers, which might remain from recipes in the other chapters in this book.

Included here with the egg dishes are a few pizza recipes, without which a garlic book would never be complete.

Garlic Scrambled Eggs

Serves 4 ──────────────(2)

---

2 large cloves garlic, preferably fresh spring garlic, peeled and thinly sliced

---

1 tablespoon butter

---

8 eggs, beaten in a bowl

---

1 teaspoon milk

Sea salt and freshly ground black pepper

Fresh chopped parsley, for garnish

---

1. In a large, heavy-bottomed frying pan heat butter and sauté garlic over low heat 5 to 10 minutes, until golden but not browned.

2. Beat eggs in a bowl with milk, salt, and pepper.

3. There should still be plenty of butter in the pan, but if there isn't add a little more and pour in eggs. The heat should be very low and eggs should scramble slowly.

4. Stir eggs slowly with garlic until they reach the state you prefer, creamy or stiff. Serve garnished with parsley, and with a salad or vegetable and bread.

Tortilla Española

Serves 4 to 6

This is a flat omelette that can be served hot or cold.

½ pound new or boiling potatoes, scrubbed and diced small
2 tablespoons olive oil
1 small onion, chopped
1-2 cloves garlic, minced or put through a press
1 sweet green pepper, seeds and membranes removed, cut in strips
1 sweet red pepper, seeds and membranes removed, cut in strips
8 eggs, beaten
Sea salt and freshly ground black pepper, to taste
2 tablespoons chopped fresh parsley or basil

1. Steam potatoes 10 minutes, until crisp-tender. Refresh under cold water and dry in a towel. Heat broiler.

2. In a 10-inch, well-seasoned or non-stick frying pan heat 1 tablespoon of oil and sauté onion and garlic until onion softens.

3. Add peppers and continue to sauté, stirring, about 5 minutes. Add potatoes and sauté another 5 minutes, or until they are soft.

4. Beat eggs in a bowl. Stir in salt and pepper to taste, and parsley or basil. Add a little more oil to pan and pour in eggs. Tilt pan so that eggs cover the surface evenly.

5. Let set while very gently shaking pan and lifting edges every now and again to let uncooked egg run underneath.

6. When omelette is just about cooked through place pan under broiler to finish, which should take about 3 minutes. It will puff up and brown a little. Serve hot or cool, cut in wedges.

Tomato Omelette

Serves 2 to 3

---

2 tablespoons butter

¾ pound tomatoes, seeded and chopped

1 clove garlic, minced or put through a press

Sea salt and freshly ground black pepper, to taste

1 teaspoon chopped fresh basil or tarragon

4 eggs, beaten

1 teaspoon milk

---

1. Heat half the butter in a frying pan and add tomatoes and garlic. Cook together 15 minutes over medium heat.

2. Season to taste with salt and freshly ground pepper and chopped fresh basil or tarragon. Remove from heat.

3. Heat rest of butter in an omelette pan while you beat eggs in a bowl. Beat in teaspoon of milk and a little salt and pepper.

4. As soon as butter stops sizzling, pour eggs into omelette pan and swirl pan. Shake pan gently as you lift edges of omelette and allow eggs to run underneath.

5. When omelette is solid enough to fold, place tomatoes in a line down the center and fold omelette, either by jerking pan quickly away from you then towards you, so that eggs flip over, or by folding with a spatula, whichever is the most comfortable for you.

6. Cook a few more minutes, depending on how runny you like your omelettes, and turn out onto a warm serving dish.

7. This can also be made in two batches in a smaller omelette pan and turned out directly onto the plates.

Mushroom and Cheese Omelette

Serves 2 to 3

---

2 tablespoons butter

½ pound mushrooms, cleaned, trimmed, and sliced thin

1 clove garlic, minced or put through a press

¼ teaspoon thyme

¼ teaspoon crushed rosemary

1 tablespoon dry white wine

Salt and freshly ground black pepper, to taste

4 eggs, beaten

1 teaspoon milk

2 ounces grated Gruyère or Parmesan cheese

Fresh chopped parsley, for garnish

1. Heat half the butter in a frying pan and add mushrooms and garlic.

2. Cook over moderate heat 5 minutes, or until mushrooms begin to soften.

3. Add thyme, rosemary, and white wine and continue to sauté another 5 minutes, or until liquid evaporates.

4. Season to taste with salt and freshly ground pepper, remove from heat, and set aside.

5. Heat remaining butter in an omelette pan, and beat eggs and milk in a bowl. Make omelette as instructed in the Tomato Omelette (page 146), filling with sautéed mushrooms and grated cheese. Turn onto a platter or plates, garnish with parsley, and serve.

Poached Eggs and Garlic
Serves 4 ③

12 large cloves garlic
1 teaspoon butter
4-8 slices whole grain bread, toasted
4-8 eggs, as desired
1 teaspoon vinegar

1. Combine garlic and about 3 cups water in a saucepan and bring to a simmer. Simmer for 15 minutes, or until garlic is soft.

2. Remove garlic from water and mash with butter. Spread on slices of toast and keep warm in oven.

3. Bring same pot of water back to a simmer and add vinegar. Poach eggs, one or a few at a time. Break them into a teacup, lower teacup into water, count to 20, then gently turn egg into simmering water. Count to 20 and turn egg over with a long-handled spoon.

4. Simmer 3 to 4 minutes, to taste. Remove from water with a slotted spoon, dip into a bowl of water to rinse off vinegar and stop the cooking, and place on toast. Serve at once.

Poached Eggs à la Provençale

Serves 4 — ②

1 tablespoon olive oil or butter
1 large clove garlic, chopped (or more, to taste)
1 shallot, chopped
2 pounds ripe tomatoes, chopped
¼ teaspoon thyme
Sea salt and freshly ground black pepper, to taste
2-3 teaspoons fresh chopped basil
4-8 eggs
2 ounces Parmesan cheese, grated

1. Preheat oven to 400°F.

2. Heat oil in a heavy-bottomed frying pan and add garlic and shallot. Sauté until golden over low heat and add tomatoes, thyme, and a little salt.

3. Simmer 20 minutes, stirring occasionally, and add basil and freshly ground pepper.

4. Meanwhile poach eggs according to directions in Poached Garlic and Eggs (page 148) but only poach 3 minutes.

5. Transfer tomato sauce to a wide, low baking dish and place eggs on top of mixture.

6. Sprinkle each egg with a little Parmesan, and place in oven about 3 minutes, or just until Parmesan melts. Serve at once.

Provençal Pizza

For the crust:

½ pound whole wheat pastry flour

½ teaspoon sea salt

1 teaspoon baking powder

½ teaspoon baking soda

½ cup water, as needed

2 tablespoons olive oil

For the topping:

2 pounds tomatoes, seeded and chopped

1 tablespoon olive oil

**1 large clove garlic, minced or put through a press
(or more to taste)**

½-1 teaspoon marjoram, to taste

¼-½ teaspoon thyme, to taste

2 ounces grated Gruyère cheese

A handful of imported black olives

2 ounces sliced mushrooms

2 tablespoons olive oil

1. Mix together flour, salt, baking powder, and baking soda. Add water and work in with your hands, then add olive oil and work in.

2. Oil a 10-inch pie pan or pizza pan with olive oil. Roll out crust ¼-inch thick and line pan.

3. Pinch a lip around the edge of the crust. Refrigerate until ready to assemble the pizza.

4. Heat 1 tablespoon olive oil in a heavy-bottomed frying pan or saucepan and sauté garlic 1 minute.

5. Add tomatoes and cook over a medium flame ½ hour, stirring occasionally.

6 Remove from heat and put through medium blade of a food mill. Season to taste with salt and pepper.

7. Preheat oven to 450°F. Spread tomato purée over pizza crust, then

sprinkle with marjoram and thyme, grated Gruyère, olives, and mushrooms. Drizzle remaining olive oil over all.

8.   Bake 15 minutes in preheated oven and serve. This freezes well.

Pissaladière
(Provençal Onion Pizza)
Serves 6 ②

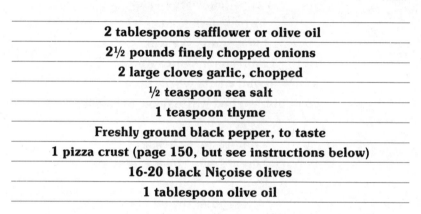

2 tablespoons safflower or olive oil

2½ pounds finely chopped onions

2 large cloves garlic, chopped

½ teaspoon sea salt

1 teaspoon thyme

Freshly ground black pepper, to taste

1 pizza crust (page 150, but see instructions below)

16-20 black Niçoise olives

1 tablespoon olive oil

1.   Heat oil in a large, heavy-bottomed saucepan and add onions, garlic, salt, and thyme.

2.   Sauté over low heat, covered, 1½-2 hours, or until onions are reduced to a purée. Stir often. Add freshly ground pepper and adjust salt.

3.   When onions are done, tilt casserole and press onions to one side so that juice runs to the other. Remove juice and set aside for crust.

4.   Make pizza crust, substituting ¼ cup of juice for water in pizza recipe instructions. Roll out and line an oiled 10-inch quiche pan or pizza pan.

5.   Preheat oven to 450°F.

6.   Spread onion mixture over crust. Decorate with olives. Drizzle on a tablespoon of olive oil. Bake 15 minutes in preheated oven, or until crust is nicely browned. Serve hot.

Calzones

Serves 8 to 10 ———————————— ③

Calzones are the Italian version of a turnover, a filling in a folded, sealed crust. You could fill them with any number of things. The one I've chosen here is a goat cheese filling seasoned with garlic and herbs.

For the crust:

1 tablespoon active dry yeast

1¼ cups lukewarm water

½ teaspoon honey

2 teaspoons sea salt

3 tablespoons olive oil

½ pound whole wheat flour

½ pound unbleached white flour, as needed

For the filling:

½ pound goat cheese

½ pound mozzarella cheese, grated

1 teaspoon crushed rosemary

1 teaspoon thyme

2 teaspoons chopped fresh sage (omit if not available)

Freshly ground black pepper

2 cloves garlic, minced or put through a press

3 tablespoons plain low-fat yogurt

1 egg, beaten

For the glaze:

4 tablespoons olive oil

2 cloves garlic, minced or put through a press

1. Dissolve yeast in water and add honey. Let sit for 10 minutes, or until it begins to bubble.

2. Stir in salt and oil. Add whole wheat flour and stir well. Add unbleached flour, ½ cup at a time, until you can turn out the dough.

3. Turn out dough onto a floured work surface and knead 10 minutes, adding more flour as necessary. Dough should be slightly sticky.

4. Oil bowl and place dough in it, seam side up first, then seam side down. Cover and place in a warm spot to rise for 1 to 1½ hours, or until doubled in bulk.

5. Meanwhile prepare filling. Sauté garlic gently in olive oil a minute or two.

6. Add to goat cheese in a bowl, and mash together with mozzarella and herbs. Blend in yogurt and egg. Add freshly ground pepper to taste.

7. Preheat oven to 400°F.

8. Punch down dough and turn it out onto work surface, which you should dust with unbleached flour. Cut dough in half to facilitate rolling out.

9. Roll out to a thickness of ¼ inch. Using a small bowl as a guide, cut into circles about 6 inches in diameter.

10. Combine garlic and olive oil for glaze. Brush each circle with this mixture and top with 2 heaping tablespoons of the filling.

11. Fold dough over filling, pinch edges together tightly, then pinch and twist a lip around the edge. Brush with garlic and olive oil mixture and place on an oiled baking sheet.

12. Bake in preheated oven 10 to 15 minutes, or until brown and crisp. Brush with oil halfway through baking and immediately upon removing from the oven. Serve at once. These freeze well.

Whole Wheat Pie Crust

Enough for 1 large quiche or 2 smaller pies

6 ounces butter

½ pound whole wheat pastry flour

½ teaspoon sea salt, unless using salted butter

Approx. 3 tablespoons ice-cold water

1. Combine flour and salt.

2. Cut butter into flour. Work between palms of hands until you have a mixture that resembles oatmeal or coarse cornmeal.

3. Add a tablespoon or two of water and gather up into a ball. If very crumbly add a little more water.

4. Wrap in plastic wrap and refrigerate 1 hour.

5. Soften with a rolling pin and roll out dough on a lightly floured work surface to a thickness of ¼ inch or less. Line a large quiche pan or two smaller pie pans. Refrigerate until ready to bake.

6. Before filling, weight by covering with a piece of foil and spreading dry beans over the surface. Prebake 5 minutes at 350°F.

Mushroom Tart

Serves 6 to 8 ———①

This can be made in advance and reheated just before serving. It can also be frozen.

1 Whole Wheat Pie Crust (above)

1 large onion, chopped

2 tablespoons safflower oil

1 tablespoon butter

1½ pounds mushrooms, large ones if possible, cleaned, trimmed, and cut in half if small or medium, or in quarters if large

1 large clove garlic, minced or put through a press

¼ teaspoon thyme, to taste

¼ teaspoon crushed rosemary, to taste

Sea salt and freshly ground black pepper, to taste

3 tablespoons dry white wine

1 teaspoon soy sauce

3 eggs

¾ cup low-fat milk

4 ounces Gruyère cheese, grated

1. Make Pie Crust and line a 10-inch quiche pan. Chill until ready to use. Preheat oven to 350°F and prebake for minutes. Set aside.

2. Brown onion in half the safflower oil. Set aside.

3. Heat butter and remaining oil in a large, heavy-bottomed frying pan and add mushrooms. Sauté, stirring, until mushrooms begin to soften and release liquid.

4. Add garlic, thyme, rosemary, salt, and a generous amount of pepper and sauté 2 to 3 minutes. Add the wine and continue to sauté until wine is absorbed.

5. Add soy sauce and stir together. Stir in browned onions, and remove from heat.

6. Beat together eggs and milk. Toss together mushrooms and cheese.

7. Fill prebaked pie crust with mushroom mixture and pour in milk and egg mixture.

8. Bake in preheated oven 30 minutes, or until firm and browning on top. Remove from heat and serve, or cool and reheat just before serving.

Tomato and Garlic Quiche

Serves 6 ②

---

1 Whole Wheat Pie Crust (page 154)

1 tablespoon butter or safflower oil

3 large cloves garlic, minced

1 pound ripe tomatoes, peeled and chopped

1 additional tomato, sliced

1 tablespoon tomato paste

¼-½ teaspoon thyme, to taste

Sea salt and freshly ground black pepper, to taste

3 large eggs, at room temperature

⅔ cup milk

4 ounces grated Gruyère cheese

1 ounce freshly grated Parmesan cheese

1. Prepare crust and prebake 5 minutes at 350°F.

2. Heat oil or butter in a heavy-bottomed frying pan and sauté garlic very slowly 1 minute.

3. Add chopped tomatoes, but not the sliced one, and tomato paste, and cook over low heat until reduced to a fairly thick paste.

4. Add thyme and season to taste with salt and freshly ground pepper. Simmer another 5 minutes and remove from heat.

5. Blend together eggs and milk and stir in tomato sauce.

6. Line prebaked pie crust with sliced tomato and top with cheeses. Pour on custard mixture.

7. Bake 30 to 40 minutes in preheated oven, or until a knife when inserted comes out clean.

8. Let sit for about 10 minutes before serving. This can also be frozen.

Onion and Potato Gratin
Serves 6 ──────────── ②

---

2 tablespoons safflower oil

1½ pounds onions, peeled and thinly sliced

2 cloves garlic, minced or put through a press

1 pound peeled and grated potatoes

½ teaspoon thyme

2 tablespoons chopped parsley

Pinch of cayenne

4 eggs

½ cup milk

3 ounces grated Gruyère cheese

Sea salt and freshly ground black pepper, to taste

1. Preheat oven to 375°F. Butter a 1- to 2-quart gratin or baking dish.

2. Heat one tablespoon of oil in a large, heavy-bottomed frying pan and sauté onions with garlic over medium-low heat about 15 minutes, or until completely soft but not browned. Remove from heat.

3. Add the other tablespoon of oil, squeeze out all the moisture from grated potatoes, and add to pan. Sauté about 5 minutes, stirring. They should just begin to get soft.

4. Remove from heat and add to onions, along with thyme and parsley. Add a pinch of cayenne.

5. Beat together eggs and milk and stir into onion mixture with grated cheese. Add salt and freshly ground pepper to taste, and transfer to prepared baking dish.

6. Bake in preheated oven 40 minutes, or until top is browned. Serve at once. This can be frozen.

Garlic Soufflé

Despite its name this Garlic Soufflé does not reek of garlic. It is a rich cheese soufflé infused with garlic purée, which you obtain by baking the foil-wrapped garlic for a long time in the oven. It is a subtle masterpiece, one you won't soon forget and well worth the effort. This recipe is inspired by Alice Waters of Chez Panisse.

2 large heads garlic
2 tablespoons olive oil
1½ teaspoons thyme
Sea salt and freshly ground black pepper
1½ cups milk
1 onion, quartered
3 cloves unpeeled garlic
1 bay leaf
2 sprigs parsley
10 black peppercorns
2 ounces butter
1 ounce unbleached white flour
5 eggs, separated
4 ounces Gruyère cheese, grated
4 ounces freshly grated Parmesan cheese
Sea salt and freshly ground black pepper, to taste
Pinch of cayenne
Butter for the soufflé dishes

1. Preheat oven to 325°F. Cut a large double-thickness square of aluminum foil and place whole heads of garlic on it. Drizzle olive oil over garlic and sprinkle with a little of the thyme, salt, and pepper.

2. Wrap in foil, sealing edges tightly but leaving some space around garlic. Place this foil envelope in oven and bake 1½ hours, or until garlic is very soft.

3. Remove from foil and allow to cool. Turn up oven to 450°F.

4. While garlic is baking combine milk, onion, 3 cloves of unpeeled garlic,

bay leaf, the rest of the thyme, parsley, and peppercorns in the top part of a double boiler and simmer above boiling water (you can also do this in a pan over a heat diffuser) 1 hour.

5. Strain and measure out 1⅓ cups. If this is not enough because of evaporation, add a little plain milk. Return to pot and keep hot.

6. When garlic is cool enough to handle, squeeze out of skins and purée through a strainer. Stir into milk.

7. Heat butter in a heavy-bottomed saucepan and add flour. Stir together over low heat, and cook roux a few minutes, stirring all the while with a wooden spoon.

8. Remove from heat and whisk in hot milk all at once. Return to heat and cook, stirring with a whisk, until thick and smooth.

9. Let simmer in a double boiler or over a heat diffuser while you prepare eggs and cheese.

10. Grate Gruyère and combine with half the Parmesan. Separate eggs and beat egg whites until stiff.

11. Butter either 8 individual ramekins or a low, 2-inch gratin dish. Dust with half the remaining Parmesan.

12. Remove sauce from heat and stir in egg yolks, one at a time. Adjust salt, add a little cayenne and pepper, and fold mixture into beaten egg whites along with cheese.

13. Carefully spoon this into prepared soufflé dishes, and sprinkle remaining Parmesan and thyme over tops.

14. Bake in hot oven for 10 minutes, and serve immediately. It should be brown on top and creamy inside.

Note: If using a normal straight sided soufflé dish, bake 20 minutes.

Spinach Timbale

Serves 6 to 8

2 ounces whole wheat bread crumbs
2 pounds fresh spinach, washed, stems removed
1 tablespoon butter or safflower oil
½ onion, finely chopped
1 clove garlic, minced or put through a press
3 ounces Gruyère cheese, grated
2 ounces Parmesan cheese, grated
Sea salt and freshly ground black pepper, to taste
4 eggs, beaten
1 cup milk
Pinch of nutmeg

1. Preheat oven to 325°F. Butter a soufflé dish and dust with a quarter of the bread crumbs.

2. Wash spinach and, while still wet, wilt in a dry frying pan. Rinse under cold water and squeeze dry in a towel. Chop fine.

3. Heat butter or oil in a large frying pan and add onion and garlic.

4. When onion is tender, add spinach and sauté a few more minutes, or until spinach is coated with butter or oil. Remove from heat and place in a bowl.

5. Toss with remaining bread crumbs, cheeses, and salt and pepper to taste.

6. Beat eggs in a bowl. Heat milk in a saucepan until it begins to tremble.

7. Remove from heat and whisk into eggs. Stir into spinach mixture and add a little nutmeg.

8. Pour this into soufflé dish and place in a pan of water. Bake in preheated oven 40 to 50 minutes, or until solid.

9. Remove from heat, let sit 10 to 15 minutes, and carefully unmold onto a serving plate. This can be frozen.

CHAPTER VIII

SAUCES AND DRESSINGS

The recipes that follow can be divided into two groups: the cooked and the raw. When garlic is cooked, as we know, its flavor becomes less pungent, although the degree of pungency will be determined by how long the garlic is cooked and how much is called for in the recipe. The first tomato sauce is quite potent, but the next three are fairly mild. The sauces that include simmered garlic are savory mixtures that will go well with vegetables and grains.

The uncooked sauces and dressings distinguish the unconditional garlic lovers. Not that these are all terribly strong, with the exception of the Aïoli, which is extremely pungent; but they are for people who, like me, like the taste of garlic in any form, whether raw or cooked.

Tomato Sauce I: Rich Tomato Sauce

Makes 1 quart ③

---

1 tablespoon olive oil

1 large onion, chopped

4 large cloves garlic, minced or put through a press (or more to taste)

1 small carrot, minced

3 pounds tomatoes, seeded and chopped

6-12 ounces tomato paste, to taste

1 bay leaf

1 teaspoon dried basil or 1 tablespoon fresh, chopped

1-2 teaspoons oregano, to taste

Sea salt and freshly ground black pepper, to taste

Pinch of cinnamon

1. Heat oil in a heavy-bottomed saucepan and sauté onion, 2 cloves of garlic, and carrot until onion is tender.

2. Add tomatoes, remaining garlic, tomato purée, and bay leaf and bring to a simmer.

3. Simmer, covered, 1 to 2 hours, stirring occasionally. Remove bay leaf and add basil and oregano.

4. Simmer another 15 minutes and add salt and freshly ground pepper to taste and a pinch or two of cinnamon. (Add more garlic if desired.)

5. This is good for lasagnes, pizzas, and lusty pasta dishes. It freezes well.

Tomato Sauce II: Quick, Light Tomato Sauce

Makes 1 quart ②

---

1 tablespoon olive oil or butter

½ onion, finely minced
2 cloves garlic, minced or put through a press
3 pounds fresh ripe tomatoes, seeded and chopped or coarsely puréed, or use the equivalent canned (a better choice if your tomatoes are not absolutely ripe)
1 tablespoon tomato paste (optional)
1 tablespoon chopped fresh basil
Pinch of cinnamon
Sea salt and freshly ground black pepper, to taste

1. Heat olive oil or butter in a heavy-bottomed saucepan or wide frying pan and sauté onion and garlic slowly over low heat 5 minutes, or until onion is translucent and garlic fragrant.

2. Add tomatoes and tomato paste and bring to a simmer. Turn up heat and cook quickly 20 minutes, stirring from time to time.

3. Add salt and pepper to taste, basil, and a pinch of cinnamon. Serve with pasta or grains. This can be frozen.

Tomato Sauce III: Light Tomato Sauce with Lots of Basil and Garlic

—— *Makes 2½ cups* —— ③

2 pounds tomatoes, peeled, seeded, and coarsely chopped
4 tablespoons fresh basil leaves, chopped
5 large cloves garlic, minced or put through a press
1 tablespoon olive oil
Sea salt and freshly ground black pepper

1. Combine all ingredients in a saucepan and simmer 30 minutes. Serve with homemade pasta, thin spaghetti, or ravioli. This can be frozen.

Tomato Sauce IV: Tomato Coulis

Makes 2½ cups — ①

2 pounds tomatoes, cut in half lengthwise

1 clove garlic, minced or put through a press

1 onion, cut in half

2 tablespoons butter

Sea salt, to taste

Pinch of cinnamon

1. Simmer tomatoes in a lidded, heavy-bottomed saucepan 10 minutes.
2. Purée through a food mill and return to pan. Add butter, onion, garlic, and salt.
3. Cook at a slow, steady simmer 1 hour. Add a pinch of cinnamon and discard onion. Adjust salt.
4. Serve with vegetables, thin pasta, grains, or ravioli.

Tomato Sauce V: Piquant Tomato Sauce

Makes 1 quart — ②

3 pounds tomatoes, fresh or canned, puréed

1 tablespoon olive or safflower oil

2 large cloves garlic, minced or put through a press

½-1 teaspoon crushed dried red pepper

1 tablespoon chopped fresh basil or 1 teaspoon dried

Sea salt, to taste

1. Purée tomatoes coarsely in a food processor, blender, or through a food mill.

2. Heat oil in a large, heavy-bottomed saucepan or frying pan and gently sauté garlic until it begins to turn color — 1 or 2 minutes.

3. Add remaining ingredients and bring to a simmer. Cook, uncovered, over moderate heat, stirring occasionally, 20 to 30 minutes.

4. Adjust salt. Serve with pasta, omelettes, vegetables, or grains. This can be frozen.

Garlicky Tomato and Caper Sauce

Serves 4 to 6

---

1 tablespoon olive oil

1 small or ½ medium onion, finely chopped

1 cup capers, chopped in a food processor or mashed in a mortar and pestle

1 small head garlic, cloves separated and peeled, then put through a press or chopped and blended with the capers in a food processor or mortar and pestle

2½ pounds tomatoes, chopped

Freshly ground black pepper, to taste

---

1. Heat olive oil in a large, heavy-bottomed frying pan and add onion.

2. Sauté a few minutes and add garlic and capers. Sauté, stirring, 5 minutes, and add tomatoes.

3. Cook over a moderate heat, stirring occasionally, ½ hour. Season to taste with freshly ground pepper.

4. Serve this with pasta, such as fettuccini or tagliatelli, or as an accompaniment to zucchini.

Egg-Lemon Sauce

Makes 1 cup ②

½ cup Garlic Broth (page 61)

3 tablespoons lemon juice, freshly squeezed

2 egg yolks

Sea salt and freshly ground black pepper, to taste

---

1. Simmer Garlic Broth.
2. Beat egg yolks in a bowl with a whisk until thick and lemon-colored. Whisk in lemon juice.
3. Remove broth from heat and whisk into egg yolks.
4. Transfer to top of a double boiler and stir over boiling water until sauce thickens. This will take about 5 to 10 minutes. It should be creamy and coat the sides of a spoon.
5. Excellent with grains or as a substitute for Hollandaise sauce with vegetables like artichokes, asparagus, and broccoli.

Creamy Garlic Sauce

Serves 6 ②

---

15 cloves garlic, peeled and left whole

1 cup water

1 vegetable bouillon cube

Pinch of thyme

Pinch of sage

1 cup plain yogurt

2 tablespoons chopped fresh parsley

Sea salt and freshly ground black pepper, to taste

Fresh lemon juice (optional)

---

1. Combine garlic, water, bouillon cube, sage, and thyme in a saucepan and simmer uncovered 30 to 40 minutes.

2. Remove from heat and purée in a blender until smooth. Add yogurt and
   mix well.

3. Stir in parsley, salt and pepper to taste, and if you wish, some lemon juice.
   Serve with vegetables or grains.

Pesto

Serves 6

If you've never had this heady mixture of basil, garlic, and cheese be prepared
for a taste treat that will change your life. It is traditionally tossed with pasta,
but I like it as a topping for tomatoes, as well as potatoes and other vegetables.
This keeps in the refrigerator for about a week, and you can freeze it by omitting
the cheese and adding it when thawed.

---

1 tightly packed cup fresh basil leaves

2 large cloves garlic, peeled

3 tablespoons pine nuts or broken walnuts

A little sea salt

½ cup olive oil

3 ounces freshly grated Parmesan cheese (or more, to taste)

---

1. Using a blender or food processor, combine basil, garlic, salt, and nuts
   and pulse several times to begin chopping and blending ingredients.
   Scrape blades often.

2. Now turn on machine at high speed and add olive oil in a slow, steady
   stream. Blend until you have a smooth paste. You may have to stop
   blender and clean blades occasionally.

3. Transfer mixture to a bowl and stir in Parmesan. Adjust seasonings.

4. This can also be made in a mortar and pestle. Pound together basil, garlic,
   salt, and nuts until you have a paste, then blend in olive oil a little at a
   time, and stir in cheese.

White Wine Sauce
Makes 2 cups ②

1⅓ cups water

8 cloves garlic, peeled and left whole

1 cup dry white wine

Sea salt, to taste

5-6 dried black Chinese mushrooms

3 tablespoons butter

3 tablespoons unbleached white or whole wheat pastry flour

Freshly ground black pepper

1. Combine water, garlic, white wine, salt, and dried mushrooms in a saucepan and bring to a simmer. Simmer uncovered 30 minutes. Strain and retain liquid.

2. Discard garlic. Rinse mushrooms, remove their tough stems, and slice caps into slivers. Set aside.

3. Heat butter in a heavy-bottomed saucepan over low heat and stir in flour. Cook, stirring with a wooden spoon, a couple of minutes, and just before mixture begins to brown whisk in hot broth and wine mixture.

4. Continue to whisk over medium heat until sauce thickens. Let simmer over low heat 10 minutes, stirring often. Taste and adjust salt.

5. Add freshly ground pepper, and if you wish, stir in slivered mushrooms (or you can use these in something else). Serve over grains, vegetables, crêpes, or soufflés. This can be frozen.

May *we have your comments on* (PLEASE PRINT TITLE OF BOOK)

Title: _____

WE HOPE THAT YOU HAVE ENJOYED THIS BOOK AND THAT IT WILL OCCUPY
A SPECIAL PLACE IN YOUR LIBRARY. WE WOULD BE MOST GRATEFUL IF YOU
WOULD FILL OUT AND MAIL THIS POSTAGE FREE CARD TO US.

Your comments: _____

_____

_____

How did this book come to your attention? _____

Your business or profession: _____

AS SOON AS WE RECEIVE THIS CARD WE WILL SEND YOU
FREE INFORMATION ABOUT OUR PUBLICATIONS.

Mr./Mrs./Miss _____

Address _____

City/State/Zip _____

MORE THAN 200 BOOKS AND TAPE ALBUMS LISTED IN THE SUMMIT LIGHTHOUSE
CATALOG ARE AVAILABLE AT OR THROUGH YOUR LOCAL BOOKSTORE.

Printed in the U.S.A.

BUSINESS REPLY CARD

FIRST CLASS   PERMIT NO. 136   MALIBU, CA

POSTAGE WILL BE PAID BY ADDRESSEE

THE SUMMIT LIGHTHOUSE
Box A
Malibu, CA 90265-9988

Aïoli: Strong Garlic Mayonnaise from Provence

———————— *Makes 2 cups* ———————— ③

2 egg yolks, at room temperature
5 cloves garlic, peeled
Sea salt, to taste
⅔ cup mild-tasting olive oil
⅔ cup safflower oil (or use all safflower oil)
Juice of 1 large lemon
Freshly ground black pepper

Using a mortar and pestle:
1. Place egg yolks in mortar and squeeze in garlic through a garlic press. Add salt to taste and blend mixture together with pestle until you have a paste.

2. Combine oils and drizzle in by the tablespoon, stirring vigorously with pestle after each addition until all the oil is incorporated and you have a smooth, thick mayonnaise.

3. Add lemon juice and pepper and continue to stir vigorously until mayonnaise is uniform. Note that what might appear as lumps are just little pieces of garlic. Do not be alarmed by how garlicky this is; it's supposed to be.

Blender or food processor Aïoli:
1. Place egg yolks in a blender jar or food processor bowl. Squeeze in garlic through a press. Add salt.

2. Turn on machine and very slowly drizzle in the oil in a thin, steady stream. You may have to stop and start blender occasionally and give mixture a stir.

3. Add lemon juice and pepper and mix well.

4. Refrigerate until ready to serve. Use as a dip with vegetables (page 89).

Garlic Tofu Mayonnaise
———————— Makes 1¼ cups ———————— ③

---

2 tablespoons lemon juice

2 tablespoons wine or cider vinegar

2 cloves garlic, minced or put through a press

1 teaspoon Dijon mustard

½ cup plain low-fat yogurt

½ pound tofu

2 teaspoons soy sauce

Pinch of cayenne

1 tablespoon safflower oil

---

1. Combine all ingredients in a blender or food processor and blend until completely smooth.

2. Refrigerate in a covered container. Use as a salad dressing or in place of mayonnaise as a dip or spread.

Variation:

Green Tofu Mayonnaise
———————— Makes 1½ cups ———————— ③

1. To the ingredients above add ½ cup chopped, fresh parsley or blanched spinach that has been squeezed dry.

2. Blend these ingredients with tofu mayonnaise mixture until smooth.

Mild Vinaigrette
Serves 6 ——————————— ②

Juice of 1 lemon

1 tablespoon vinegar

1 small clove garlic, puréed or put through a press

½ teaspoon Dijon mustard (optional)

¼ teaspoon tarragon

¼ teaspoon basil or marjoram

Sea salt and freshly ground black pepper, to taste

½ cup safflower oil, olive oil, or a combination

1. Stir together lemon juice, vinegar, garlic, optional mustard, herbs, salt, and pepper.
2. Whisk in oil. Toss with salad of your choice.

Yogurt Vinaigrette with Goat Cheese
Serves 6 ——————————— ②

Juice of ½ lemon

2 tablespoons red wine vinegar

1 small clove garlic, minced or put through a press

½ teaspoon Dijon mustard

Sea salt and freshly ground black pepper, to taste

3 ounces crumbled goat cheese

½ cup plain low-fat yogurt

1. Mix together lemon juice, wine vinegar, garlic, mustard, salt, and pepper.
2. Add goat cheese and yogurt and mix well. Toss with salad of your choice.

Garlic Vinaigrette
Serves 4 ─── ③

2-3 tablespoons good wine vinegar
2 cloves garlic, puréed or put through a press
1 teaspoon Dijon mustard
1 teaspoon fresh chopped herbs, such as tarragon, basil, thyme, parsley, marjoram or teaspoon dried tarragon and marjoram
Sea salt and freshly ground black pepper, to taste
⅓ cup minus 1 T good virgin olive oil

1. Combine vinegar, garlic, mustard, herbs, salt, and pepper and mix well.
2. Stir in oil and blend well. Toss with salad just before serving.

Variation:

Vinaigrette Made with Garlic Vinegar
Serves 4 ─── ①

This is a much milder vinaigrette. Rather than including fresh garlic in the dressing itself, keep a bottle of wine vinegar on hand in which 1 to 3 cloves of garlic, cut in half, have been submerged for at least a day and preferably longer. Follow the above recipe, omitting the crushed garlic. You may also substitute lemon juice for some of the vinegar.

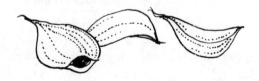

Green Gazpacho Dressing

Serves 6

②

2 tablespoons coarsely chopped onion

1 clove garlic, peeled

½ green pepper, seeds removed, cut into quarters

1 tablespoon fresh basil

2 sprigs parsley

½ teaspoon tarragon

½ pound ripe tomatoes, quartered

Juice of 1 large lemon

2 tablespoons wine vinegar

3 tablespoons olive oil

Sea salt and freshly ground black pepper, to taste

1. Purée all ingredients in a blender until smooth. Chill until ready to use. Use for salads and vegetables.

Spicy Chinese Salad Dressing

Serves 6 ──②

This is good for cold noodles, bean sprouts, and shredded vegetables.

3 tablespoons tahini
2 tablespoons soy sauce
4 tablespoons cider vinegar or white wine vinegar
1 dried hot cayenne pepper (a very small one)
2 tablespoons sesame oil
2 tablespoons safflower oil
1 tablespoon finely minced or grated fresh ginger
1 large clove minced garlic
1 cup plain low-fat yogurt or Vegetable Stock (page 60)

1. Combine all ingredients in a blender and blend until smooth.

CHAPTER IX

SALADS

Of course there are unending possibilities for salad combinations using the dressings in the previous chapter, beginning with something as simple as a green salad with a mild garlic vinaigrette. I have omitted the obvious in this small selection of grain and vegetable salads. Again, these are for the person who enjoys the flavor of raw garlic, which is nonetheless quite moderate in most of the recipes.

Warm Green Bean
Amandine Salad

Serves 4 to 6 ————————————— ①

1½ pounds green beans

2 ounces slivered almonds

1 tablespoon butter or safflower oil

Juice of ½ lemon

2 tablespoons red wine or champagne vinegar

½-1 teaspoon Dijon mustard, to taste

1 small clove garlic, minced or put through a press

¼ teaspoon tarragon

¼ teaspoon marjoram

½ cup olive oil, or a combination olive and safflower oil

4 tablespoons chopped fresh parsley

Sea salt and freshly ground black pepper, to taste

1. Steam green beans until just tender — about 10 minutes. Sauté almonds in butter or oil until brown.

2. Make a vinaigrette with lemon juice, vinegar, mustard, garlic, herbs, and oil.

3. When beans are done, drain and toss at once with dressing, almonds, and chopped fresh parsley. Add salt and freshly ground pepper to taste and serve at once.

Illustrated opposite.

Opposite: Tomato and Red Onion Salad with Goat's Cheese (page 177) and Warm Green Bean Salad Amandine (above).

Tomato and Red Onion Salad with Goat Cheese

Serves 4 — ②

4 large, ripe tomatoes, sliced thin
1 medium red onion, sliced in thin rings
3 ounces goat cheese, sliced
1 tablespoon red wine vinegar
1 clove garlic, minced
Sea salt and freshly ground black pepper, to taste
3-4 tablespoons fruity olive oil
Imported French olives and fresh basil, for garnish

1. Layer tomato slices attractively on a platter and top with onions and goat cheese.

2. Mix together vinegar, garlic, salt, and freshly ground pepper, and stir in olive oil.

3. Pour over salad, and garnish with basil. Scatter olives on salad and serve.

Illustrated opposite page 176.

Tabouli

Serves 6 to 8

½ pound bulgur

Juice of 2 lemons

1 clove garlic, minced or put through a press (or more, to taste)

½ teaspoon ground cumin

Sea salt to taste

½ cup olive oil

2 large, ripe tomatoes, chopped

1 cup chopped fresh parsley

1 small cucumber, peeled and chopped

4 tablespoons minced scallions

4 tablespoons chopped fresh mint

Crisp inner leaves from 1 head romaine lettuce

1. Place bulgur in a bowl and pour on three times its volume of water. Let soak 1 hour, or until soft.

2. Place a tea towel in a colander and drain bulgur. Squeeze out excess moisture in towel, and place bulgur in a bowl.

3. Mix together lemon juice, garlic, cumin, and salt to taste. Stir in olive oil and blend well.

4. Toss with bulgur, tomatoes, parsley, cucumber, minced scallions, and mint. Decorate bowl with lettuce leaves, which you can use as scoopers. This salad should be served with pita bread.

Cucumber-Yogurt Salad

Serves 6

4 tablespoons wine vinegar

Juice of ½ lemon

1 clove garlic, minced, puréed, or put through a press

1 teaspoon Dijon mustard

1 teaspoon fresh chopped herbs, such as basil, parsley, thyme

Sea salt and freshly ground black pepper, to taste

½ cup plain yogurt

2 pounds cucumbers, peeled and sliced thin

1 small red onion, sliced thin

1. Mix together vinegar, lemon juice, garlic, mustard, herbs, salt, and pepper.

2. Stir in yogurt, whisk together until you have a smooth sauce, and toss with cucumbers and onions. Chill and toss again before serving.

Cucumber & Tomato Salad in Garlic-Yogurt Dressing
Serves 6 ②

1 large cucumber or 2 smaller ones, peeled and chopped

½ pound tomatoes, chopped

4 scallions, minced

½ cup chopped fresh mint

½ cup chopped fresh parsley

Juice of 2 large lemons

2 cloves garlic, minced or put through a press

Sea salt, to taste

2 tablespoons olive oil

1 cup plain low-fat yogurt

Freshly ground black pepper

1. Toss together vegetables and herbs.

2. Stir together lemon juice, garlic, salt, olive oil, and yogurt until smooth. Grind in some pepper.

3. Toss with vegetables and serve, or chill and serve.

Marinated Cucumbers

Serves 6 to 8

---

2 large or 3-4 smaller cucumbers, peeled and cut into spears

1 white or red onion, sliced thin

¾ cup water

¾ cup white wine or cider vinegar

2 cloves garlic, minced or put through a press

Sea salt and freshly ground black pepper, to taste

2 tablespoons chopped fresh dill, or 1 tablespoon dried

4 tablespoons safflower oil

---

1. Combine onion, vinegar, water, and garlic in a saucepan and bring to a boil. Boil 1 minute and remove from heat.

2. Cool 1 minute, and add salt and pepper, dill, and oil. Pour over cucumbers and toss well.

3. Cover and refrigerate several hours, tossing from time to time.

Creamy Cucumber Salad

Serves 6

---

2 long cucumbers or 3 short cucumbers

Juice of 1 lemon

1 small clove garlic, minced or put through a press

4 tablespoons chopped fresh dill

Freshly ground black pepper, to taste

1 cup cottage cheese

½ cup plain yogurt

4 ounces goat cheese, as fresh as possible, crumbled

Sea salt, to taste

---

1. Toss cucumbers with lemon juice, garlic, and dill. Add freshly ground pepper to taste.

2. Blend together cottage cheese and yogurt in a food processor, mixer, or blender until smooth. Stir in goat cheese.

3. Toss with cucumbers. Taste again and add salt as needed. Chill until ready to serve.

Leftover Bread Salad
Serves 6 — ②

---

1 pound stale whole wheat bread

1 small red onion

1 tablespoon fresh basil, chopped

1 tablespoon fresh parsley, chopped

2 tablespoons red wine vinegar

1 clove garlic, minced or put through a press

3 large, ripe tomatoes, chopped

Sea salt and freshly ground black pepper, to taste

5 tablespoons olive oil

---

1. Place bread in a bowl and cover with cold water. Peel onion, cut in half, and place over bread. Soak 20 minutes. Drain and squeeze all the water out of the bread. Depending on bread, it may crumble, which is fine.

2. Slice onion very thin and toss with bread along with tomatoes, basil, and parsley.

3. Mix together vinegar, garlic, salt, and pepper and whisk in oil. Toss with bread, cover, and refrigerate at least 2 hours. Then serve.

4. You can also refrigerate bread, onion, tomatoes, basil, and parsley without dressing, then toss with dressing just before serving.

Warm Potato and Mushroom Salad

Serves 4 to 6

1½ pounds boiling or new potatoes, scrubbed

1 tablespoon olive oil

6 ounces cleaned and sliced mushrooms

1 large clove garlic

2 tablespoons finely chopped onion or shallot

2 tablespoons dry white wine, for the mushrooms

Sea salt and freshly ground black pepper, to taste

½ teaspoon soy sauce

3 tablespoons dry white wine, for the potatoes

1 tablespoon chopped chives

2 tablespoons finely chopped parsley

3 leaves fresh sage, chopped

2 tablespoons wine vinegar

4 tablespoons olive oil

2 tablespoons safflower oil

---

1. Steam potatoes in their skins until tender but not mushy — about 15 minutes, or longer for larger potatoes.

2. Meanwhile heat 1 tablespoon olive oil in a heavy-bottomed frying pan and sauté mushrooms with garlic and finely chopped onion or shallot 5 minutes over medium heat.

3. Add 2 tablespoons white wine, some salt and freshly ground pepper, and continue to cook until wine evaporates. Stir in soy sauce and remove from heat.

4. When potatoes are tender remove from heat, run for a moment under cold water, and immediately slice ¼ to ½ inch thick and toss with the 3 tablespoons white wine, chives, parsley, and sage.

5. Stir together vinegar and oils, toss with potatoes and mushrooms, adjust seasonings, and serve at once.

Pickled Beets

Serves 6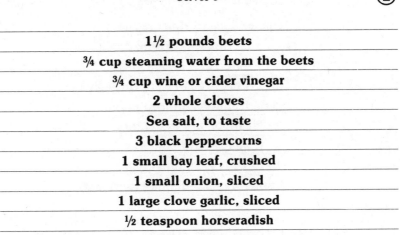

1½ pounds beets
¾ cup steaming water from the beets
¾ cup wine or cider vinegar
2 whole cloves
Sea salt, to taste
3 black peppercorns
1 small bay leaf, crushed
1 small onion, sliced
1 large clove garlic, sliced
½ teaspoon horseradish

1. Place beets in a steamer above 1 cup boiling water. Cover, reduce heat, and steam 40 minutes, or until beets are tender.

2. Check water from time to time to make sure it doesn't boil dry. Remove from steamer, run under cold water, peel, and slice thinly.

3. Measure out required amount from steaming water and combine with remaining ingredients in saucepan. Bring to a boil and add sliced beets.

4. Remove from heat, transfer to a bowl, cover, and refrigerate several hours.

Guacamole
Serves 4 to 6 ────────(2)

2 large or 3 small ripe avocados*

1 ripe tomato, chopped

Juice of 1 lemon

1 small clove garlic, puréed or put through a press

2-3 tablespoons minced onion

¼ teaspoon ground cumin

Sea salt, to taste

Lettuce leaves, for serving

Sliced tomatoes, for garnish (optional)

1. Cut avocados in half and scoop out pulp. Mash in a bowl with a pestle or wooden spoon, fork, or potato masher.

2. Add tomato and continue to mash together.

3. Stir in lemon juice, garlic, onion, cumin, and salt. Adjust seasonings (you may want a little more lemon or garlic).

4. Transfer to an attractive serving bowl. Place lettuce leaves on individual plates and serve garnished with tomato slices. This can also serve as a dip.

* Preferably the dark, gnarled-skinned variety, which are much richer and less watery than the thin-skinned kind.

Russian Salad
Serves 6 to 8 ──────────────②

---

1 pound red or boiling potatoes, washed and peeled if desired

1 small red onion, minced

½ pound diced carrots

1 pound (unshelled) fresh or frozen peas, shelled

1 medium or 2 small dill pickles, rinsed and chopped

½ cup plus 1 teaspoon mayonnaise, preferably homemade, or Garlic Tofu Mayonnaise (page 170)

For the vinaigrette:

1 tablespoon fresh lemon juice

3 tablespoons wine or cider vinegar

1 clove garlic, minced or put through a press

1 teaspoon Dijon mustard

½ teaspoon dried dill or 1 teaspoon chopped fresh dill

Sea salt and freshly ground black pepper, to taste

½ cup safflower oil

---

1. Steam potatoes until just tender — about 15 to 20 minutes (longer for larger potatoes).

2. Meanwhile make vinaigrette. Mix together lemon juice, vinegar, garlic, mustard, dill, and salt and pepper. Whisk in safflower oil.

3. When potatoes are cooked, drain, rinse under cold water, and dice. Toss immediately with vinaigrette and minced onion.

4. Steam carrots until just tender and peas until bright green and tender. Toss with potatoes.

5. Add diced pickles and mayonnaise and stir together well. Cover and chill until ready to serve.

Roasted Red Pepper Salad

—————————— *Serves 4 to 6* ——————————

2-4 large red sweet peppers

5 tablespoons olive oil

1 clove garlic, minced, puréed, or put through a press

Sea salt and freshly ground black pepper, to taste

Fresh chopped basil (optional)

1. Heat broiler and place peppers on a baking sheet close to flame. Roast, turning at regular intervals, until peppers are charred black all the way around. (This can also be done directly over a flame, turning the peppers regularly.)

2. Remove peppers from heat and place in a damp towel or in a plastic bag for 10 minutes. Peel off all of charred skin under cold water. Pat dry with paper towels.

3. Cut peppers in half, remove seeds and membranes, and cut into wide strips.

4. Mix together olive oil, garlic, salt and pepper to taste, and toss with peppers.

5. Refrigerate, covered, 1 hour before serving. Garnish, if you wish, with fresh basil.

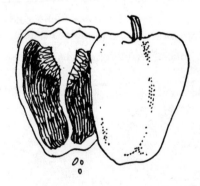

Cauliflower Vinaigrette with Peas

Serves 6 ①

---

1 red onion, sliced very thin

1 large head cauliflower, broken into florets

1 pound fresh peas, shelled (unshelled weight)

4 tablespoons chopped fresh parsley

1 tablespoon chopped fresh tarragon, if available

1 recipe Mild Vinaigrette (page 171)

---

1. Bring a large pot of water to a boil and drop in sliced onion.

2. Add cauliflower, and when water comes back to a boil, time for 2 minutes, drain. Refresh under cold water and drain on a towel.

3. Steam peas 10 minutes, or until tender but still bright green. Refresh under cold water and drain on a towel.

4. Toss vegetables and herbs together with Mild Vinaigrette and chill until ready to serve, or serve at once.

Illustrated opposite page 112.

Shredded Vegetable Salad with Spicy Chinese Dressing

Serves 6 —②

1 pound shredded cabbage

1 small or medium cucumber, peeled and shredded or cut in julienne strips

1 medium or large carrot, shredded

3 scallions, chopped

2 tablespoonsful toasted sesame seeds

1 recipe Spicy Chinese Salad Dressing (page 174)

1 head Bibb lettuce, leaves separated and washed

Chopped fresh coriander and additional sesame seeds for garnish

1. Combine all the shredded vegetables and toss with dressing.

2. Line a platter or salad bowl with lettuce leaves, and fill with shredded vegetable mixture.

3. Sprinkle top with additional sesame seeds and chopped fresh coriander, and serve.

BIBLIOGRAPHY

Harris, Lloyd G., *The Book of Garlic*. Holt, Rinehart & Winston, New York, 1974-75.

Root, Waverly, *Food*. Simon & Schuster, New York, 1980.

INDEX